T0283496

Options for Improving Strategic Utilization of the Air Reserve Component for Sustained Active-Duty Missions

AGNES GEREBEN SCHAEFER, KIMBERLY JACKSON,
MARIA MCCOLLESTER, THOMAS BUSH, LAURA KUPE,
KATHERINE L. KIDDER, PAUL EMSLIE, MICHAEL H. PHAN,
THOMAS GOUGHNOUR

Prepared for the Department of the Air Force
Approved for public release; distribution unlimited

PROJECT AIR FORCE

For more information on this publication, visit **www.rand.org/t/RRA270-1**.

About RAND

The RAND Corporation is a research organization that develops solutions to public policy challenges to help make communities throughout the world safer and more secure, healthier and more prosperous. RAND is nonprofit, nonpartisan, and committed to the public interest. To learn more about RAND, visit www.rand.org.

Research Integrity

Our mission to help improve policy and decisionmaking through research and analysis is enabled through our core values of quality and objectivity and our unwavering commitment to the highest level of integrity and ethical behavior. To help ensure our research and analysis are rigorous, objective, and nonpartisan, we subject our research publications to a robust and exacting quality-assurance process; avoid both the appearance and reality of financial and other conflicts of interest through staff training, project screening, and a policy of mandatory disclosure; and pursue transparency in our research engagements through our commitment to the open publication of our research findings and recommendations, disclosure of the source of funding of published research, and policies to ensure intellectual independence. For more information, visit www.rand.org/about/research-integrity.

RAND's publications do not necessarily reflect the opinions of its research clients and sponsors.

About This Report

Since 9/11, the United States has relied heavily on the Air Force Reserve and Air National Guard because of downsizing, reduced budgets, and the Regular Air Force's rising operational tempo. As a result, the Air Reserve Component (ARC) became essential for operations across many mission areas. The objective of this project was to (1) analyze how statutes, personnel policies, and resource policies constrain how ARC personnel are utilized to perform frequent or long-term active component operational requirements; to (2) suggest potential changes that would make accessing the ARC more efficient; and to (3) suggest specific strategic solutions for an operational ARC.

The research reported here was commissioned by the Deputy Assistant Secretary of the Air Force for Force Management Integration and conducted within the Workforce, Development and Health Program of RAND Project AIR FORCE as part of a fiscal year 2018 project titled Analysis of Personnel and Resource Policy Affecting the Total Force.

RAND Project AIR FORCE

RAND Project AIR FORCE (PAF), a division of the RAND Corporation, is the Department of the Air Force's (DAF's) federally funded research and development center for studies and analyses, supporting both the United States Air Force and the United States Space Force. PAF provides the DAF with independent analyses of policy alternatives affecting the development, employment, combat readiness, and support of current and future air, space, and cyber forces. Research is conducted in four programs: Strategy and Doctrine; Force Modernization and Employment; Resource Management; and Workforce, Development, and Health. The research reported here was prepared under contract FA7014-16-D-1000.

Additional information about PAF is available on our website: www.rand.org/paf/

This report documents work originally shared with the DAF incrementally in several briefings during 2017 and 2018. The draft report, issued on September 28, 2018, was reviewed by formal peer reviewers and DAF subject-matter experts.

The appearance of hyperlinks does not constitute endorsement by the United States Department of Defense (DoD) of the linked websites or the information, products, or services contained therein. DoD does not exercise any editorial, security, or other control over the information you may find at these locations.

Contents

Figures

Tables

Summary

Issue

Over time, the reserve components have shifted from primarily a strategic force in the mid-twentieth century to today's operational force composed of both part-time and full-time members. The aftermath of 9/11 led to an increase in the demand for U.S. military forces to project U.S. power around the globe and the emergence of the reserve components as an operational force. Yet there is inherent tension and contradiction in the operational force construct, for it insists on having reserve components—which are, by definition, a part-time force to be held in "reserve"—that are also ready for conflict at any time.

Approach

The objectives of this report are to (1) analyze how statutes, personnel policies, and resource policies constrain how Air Reserve Component (ARC) personnel are utilized to perform frequent or long-term active component operational requirements; to (2) suggest potential changes that would make accessing the ARC more efficient; and to (3) suggest specific strategic solutions for an operational ARC. The study team approached this issue using a mixed methodology consisting of focused legal and policy reviews, informational discussions with senior U.S. Air Force leaders, and an analysis of U.S. Air Force personnel data. This multifaceted approach allowed us to use various data sources and analyses to develop our recommendations to the U.S. Air Force.

Recommendations

A summary of the legal, resource, policy, and permeability constraints that we identified through our legal and policy reviews, as well as our informational discussions, can be found in Table S.1. This table also outlines

TABLE S.1

Summary of Legal, Resource, Policy, and Permeability Constraints to Air Reserve Component Utilization and Recommendations to Address Them

Constraints to ARC Utilization	Recommendations
Legal	
Duty status system	Continue to support duty status reform
Legal structure that dictates rigid funding streams for components	Enable some budget flexibility
Potential constraints placed on volunteerism by current 1,095 man-day strength accounting requirement	Realign the strength accounting requirement
Limitations on duties that FTS personnel may perform	Address the limitations placed on full-time support personnel
Resource	
Lack of adequate and predictable funding	Program sufficient operational support funding for the ARC
Volatility added to budget-planning process by continuing resolutions	Stress to lawmakers the toll that continuing resolutions have on the U.S. Air Force
Funding disconnected from end strength	Align appropriations with strength accounting
Rigidity of resource management processes	Enable some budget flexibility
Policy	
Ambiguous full-time support personnel policies	Clarify ambiguous policies
Confusion over 1,095 man-day rule	Clarify ambiguous policies
Lack of clarity on joint travel regulations	Provide flexibility in travel and housing allowances
Burdensome waiver processes	Reduce waiver requirements
Permeability	
Separate pay and benefits systems	Continue to support development of U.S. Air Force Integrated Personnel and Pay System
Challenges with reserve unit reaffiliation and career progression	Enable ARC members' career progression while on active duty
Cumbersome scrolling process	Streamline or eliminate the scrolling process
Lack of cross-component understanding	Facilitate cross-component experiences

our corresponding recommendations to address each of the identified constraints.

Conclusions

Given that the U.S. Air Force has been consumed with enduring conflicts since 9/11 and it appears that continuing need for ARC support to the Regular Air Force will not stop anytime soon, it is appropriate for the U.S. Air Force to revisit the ongoing dialogue about the purpose and appropriate employment of its ARC—especially with regard to sustained operational support to the Regular Air Force. While attention often focuses on the day-to-day constraints to utilizing the ARC, the crux of the debates about these types of constraints stems from larger questions about the appropriate employment of the ARC—particularly for sustained support to the Regular Air Force. The recommendations in this report aim to provide the U.S. Air Force with options for addressing various levels of constraints to ARC utilization for sustained operational support missions.

Acknowledgments

We would like to extend thanks to our U.S. Air Force sponsor, who provided valuable feedback on various briefings over the course of the creation of this report. In particular, we would like to thank Jeffrey Mayo. We are also grateful to our action officers, Col Michelle Barrett and CMSgt Dennis Orcutt, who were very helpful in providing oversight of this research effort.

We also note that we could not have completed this work without the support of subject-matter experts and senior military and civilian leaders from across the Air Reserve Component, Major Commands, and Headquarters Air Force. In addition, we appreciate the perspectives of individuals from the other services who provided us information on how they manage the subpopulation in their reserve components who perform frequent or long-term active-duty missions. We are grateful for their assistance with our efforts to collect information for this report.

Finally, we also greatly benefited from the contributions of our RAND colleagues, including Ray Conley and Kirsten Keller, who provided incredibly helpful feedback on this report, as well as our peer reviewers: Al Robbert, James Leftwich, and Bob Corsi.

We retain full responsibility for the objectivity, accuracy, and analytic integrity of the work presented here.

Abbreviations

ADOS	Active-Duty Operational Support
AFI	Air Force Instruction
AFR	Air Force Reserve
AFSC	Air Force Specialty Code
AGR	Active Guard Reserve
ANG	Air National Guard
ARC	Air Reserve Component
BAH-AC	Basic Allowance for Housing–Active Component
BAH-RC	Basic Allowance for Housing–Reserve Component
CCMD	combatant command
CR	continuing resolution
DoD	Department of Defense
DSG	drill status guardsman
FSS	force support squadron
FTNG	full-time National Guard
FTS	full-time support
FY	fiscal year
IMA	individual mobilization augmentee
JTR	Joint Travel Regulations
M4S	Manpower Military Personnel Appropriations Man-Day Management System
MOT	Mobilization on Tour
MPA	Military Personnel Appropriations
NCSAF	National Commission on the Structure of the Air Force
NGPA	National Guard Personnel Appropriations
O&M	Operations and Maintenance
OAIT	organize, administer, instruct, and train
OARIT	organize, administer, recruit, instruct, and train
OCO	Overseas Contingency Operations

PCS	permanent change of station
POM	Program Objective Memorandum
RC	reserve component
RegAF	Regular Air Force
RFPB	Reserve Forces Policy Board
RPA	Reserve Personnel Appropriations
SAF/MR	Assistant Secretary of the Air Force for Manpower and Reserve Affairs
TDY	temporary duty
TR	Traditional Reservist
U.S.C.	United States Code
VLPAD	Voluntary Limited Period of Active Duty

CHAPTER ONE

Introduction

Background and Study Purpose

Since 9/11, the United States has continued to rely heavily on the Air Force Reserve (AFR) and Air National Guard (ANG) because of downsizing, reduced budgets, and the Regular Air Force's (RegAF's) rising operational tempo. As a result, the Air Reserve Component (ARC) became essential for operations across many mission areas.[1] Budget constraints and subsequent end-strength reductions in fiscal year (FY) 2014 caused by sequestration further reinforced the U.S. Air Force's reliance on the AFR and ANG. To absorb end-strength reductions while maintaining current missions and prepare for future missions, the U.S. Air Force relied heavily on the flexible use of all three components. More missions continued to be shifted to the ARC, such as airborne early warning and control, air sovereignty, and remotely piloted aircraft. In addition, as a result of the U.S. Air Force's deliberate decision to place key elements of its force structure into the ARC (e.g., tankers, air mobility, and remotely piloted aircraft), these assets have been heavily relied on by the RegAF. As one senior U.S. Air Force leader told us, "Follow the equipment, not the people."[2] In other words, placing critical equipment in the ARC has facilitated the evolution of the ARC into an operational reserve.

---

[1] Office of the Vice Chairman of the Joint Chiefs of Staff and Office of the Assistant Secretary of Defense for Reserve Affairs, *Comprehensive Review of the Future Role of the Reserve Component*, Washington, D.C.: Department of Defense, 2011, p. 16.

[2] Interview AF1, senior AFR official, June 19, 2018.

As one senior U.S. Air Force leader told us, in this new era, the ARC currently resembles a triangle (Figure 1.1).[3] Most of the ARC is a strategic reserve at its foundation (meaning it serves to augment the active duty in times of war), but there is a small piece that is an operational reserve (meaning it routinely carries out operational missions). It is in this small slice of the ARC that members perform long-term, sustained, active-duty operational support missions.

This shift to the operational reserve also presents challenges. As the U.S. Air Force relies on the ARC to assist in fulfilling the U.S. Air Force's mission, the operational tempo for some ANG and AFR members has increased as well. This increased demand for ARC manpower may create challenges for the ARC in trying to recruit members from the RegAF. Heavy utilization may mean that some individuals could prefer to either remain on active duty or forgo service altogether rather than enter the ARC. It may further create retention issues for the ARC, as the operational tempo may become too high for certain members to sustain participation.

As the RegAF has become increasingly reliant on the operational slice of the ARC, there is some growing concern that current statutes, resource poli-

FIGURE 1.1

Elements of the Current Air Reserve Component

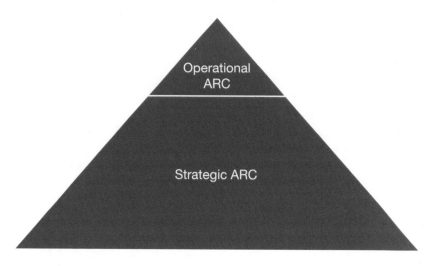

Operational ARC

Strategic ARC

---

[3] Interview AF1, senior AFR official, June 19, 2018.

cies, and personnel policies for managing the strategic reserve have become outdated in the era of the operational ARC. These concerns gave rise to the U.S. Air Force's request for RAND to examine this topic more closely. The aim of this study is to identify the legal, resource, policy, and permeability constraints on utilizing the population in the ARC that conducts sustained support to active-duty operational support missions, and to provide recommendations to address those constraints. Before we discuss our approach and findings, we first review some basic definitions of personnel categories in the ARC.

Air Reserve Component Personnel Categories

Active Duty, Full-Time National Guard Duty, and Inactive Duty

Within the ARC, there are members who serve on active duty, full-time National Guard (FTNG) duty, and inactive duty. As described later in this report, there are approximately 30 different duty statuses under which an ARC member may perform duty, but they all are based on one of these three types of duty. Both AFR and ANG members can be called or ordered to active duty under Title 10 of the United States Code (U.S.C.). The ARC complements the RegAF by supporting operations and missions assigned to the RegAF.

Active duty for the reserve components, regulated under Title 10 of the U.S.C., includes full-time training duty, annual training duty, and attendance, while in the active military service, at a school designated as a service school by law or by the secretary of the military department concerned. The term *active duty*, as defined in Title 10 of the U.S.C., does not include FTNG duty.[4]

FTNG duty is similar to active duty but is only applicable to the National Guard. When not in federal service of the United States, FTNG duty is regulated under Title 32 of the U.S.C. and is performed to conduct training and other missions assigned to the ANG in law or by the secretary of the U.S. Air Force.

---

[4] 10 U.S.C. § 101(d)(1).

Finally, AFR and ANG members both participate in inactive duty, which includes periods of readiness training, additional periods of readiness training, muster duty, and funeral honors duty. ARC members who perform annual training and participate in required periods of inactive-duty training are commonly referred to as the part-time force.

Selected Reserve and Inactive Reserve

The reserve component of the U.S. armed forces is composed of the Reserves (the Air Force Reserve, the Army Reserve, the Coast Guard Reserve, the Navy Reserve, and the Marine Corps Reserve) and the National Guard (Air National Guard of the United States and Army National Guard of the United States). Members of the reserve component are assigned to one of three categories: the Ready Reserve, the Standby Reserve, and the Retired Reserve. The Ready Reserve is the "main manpower pool of the RC [reserve component] and will usually be called to active duty before the Standby Reserve and the Retired Reserve."[5] Within the Ready Reserve, there are three distinct personnel categories: the Selected Reserve, the Individual Ready Reserve, and the Inactive National Guard.

The Selected Reserve is the portion of the reserve component that includes personnel who regularly drill and train and is composed of both part-time and full-time personnel. It also has several personnel categories within it. For the purposes of this report, we will focus on (1) Active Guard Reserve (AGR), (2) dual-status military technicians, (3) Traditional Reservists (TRs)/drill status guardsmen (DSGs), and (4) individual mobilization augmentees (IMAs). Next, we define each of these personnel categories.

Active Guard Reserve

The AGR is a personnel category found in both the AFR and the ANG. AGR members are on active duty or FTNG duty for 180 consecutive days or more for the purposes of organizing, administering, recruiting, instructing, and training (OARIT) within the ARC, or to perform other duties as prescribed

---

[5] Lawrence Kapp, *Reserve Component Personnel Issues: Questions and Answers*, Washington, D.C.: Congressional Research Service, July 2010, pp. 1–2.

in Title 10 or Title 32.[6] They are more commonly identified as an element of the full-time support (FTS) force that manages the day-to-day operations and activities of the part-time forces for the AFR or ANG.

Air Reserve Technicians/Military Technicians

Dual-status military technicians are civilian employees in the AFR (called air reserve technicians) or ANG (called military technicians) who are required, as a condition of employment, to maintain a military position as a TR or DSG, respectively.[7] These individuals are full-time civilian employees who perform duties similar to those of AGRs, supporting the day-to-day functions of organizing, administering, instructing, and training (OAIT) for their AFR or ANG organizations. Military technicians also maintain and repair supplies or equipment issued to the Selected Reserve or the armed forces (in the case of the AFR), or issued to the National Guard or armed forces (in the case of the ANG).[8] While military technicians are primarily a civilian resource, their part-time military obligation as TRs or DSGs subjects them to being available for activation should the country need to order them to active duty or FTNG duty.

Traditional Reservists and Drill Status Guardsmen

The TR (an AFR term) and DSG (an ANG term) make up the part-time force and the largest population in the ARC. They are considered the backbone of the reserve components. In this status, they are required to complete annual training and attend regularly scheduled unit training periods (inactive-duty training periods, also known as drills). Some TRs and DSGs also participate in additional training periods required to maintain individual and unit readiness requirements.[9] The general purpose of TRs and DSGs is to provide a ready strategic force should the country need to activate them.

---

[6] Department of Defense Instruction 1215.06, *Uniform Reserve, Training, and Retirement Categories for the Reserve Components*, March 11, 2014, pp. 16–18.

[7] Although the law provides for non–dual status technicians, the ANG and the AFR are no longer authorized to employ them.

[8] 10 U.S.C. § 10216; 32 U.S.C. § 709.

[9] DoDI 1215.06, 2014, p. 11.

Individual Mobilization Augmentees

IMAs are found in the AFR. These members are similar to TRs but are assigned to augment different U.S. Air Force organizations, typically above the unit level, to support mission requirements.[10] Similar to TRs, IMAs perform annual training and attend regularly scheduled training periods. Historically, IMAs have been considered an element of the strategic force available for activation.

Study Approach

If one thinks in terms of the increasing level of active-duty participation across U.S. Air Force personnel, the population within the ARC that conducts sustained operational support missions is situated between traditional ARC members (who drill once a month and conduct two weeks of annual training) and RegAF members (who are on continuous active duty). Figure 1.2 illustrates the spectrum of active-duty participation across personnel categories of ARC and RegAF members.

FIGURE 1.2

Illustration of U.S. Air Force Personnel Based on Increasing Level of Active-Duty Participation

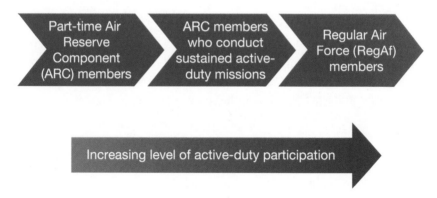

---

[10] Air Force Instruction 36-2629, *Individual Reservist Management*, August 13, 2012, para. 1.1.2.1.

The focus of this study is the middle population in the ARC, which conducts sustained active-duty missions. The objectives of this study are to (1) analyze how statutes, personnel policies, and resource policies constrain how ARC personnel are utilized to perform frequent or long-term active component operational requirements; to (2) suggest potential changes that would make accessing the ARC more efficient; and to (3) suggest specific strategic solutions for an operational ACR.

The study team approached this issue using a mixed methodology consisting of focused legal and policy reviews, informational discussions with senior U.S. Air Force leaders, and an analysis of U.S. Air Force personnel data. Our legal and policy reviews included reviews of current statutes, personnel and resource policies, and processes that constrain utilization of the ARC for sustained active-duty missions. We reviewed Department of Defense (DoD) and U.S. Air Force policies, as well as information on how the other services manage their reserve component members who provide frequent or long-term support to active component missions.

The study approach also included informational discussions with senior military and civilian U.S. Air Force personnel.[11] Discussions with these leaders focused on identifying challenges to utilizing the ARC to support active-duty missions, as well as potential solutions. We took notes during all our informational discussions and then coded this information to identify barriers to utilizing ARC members for sustained active-duty missions. We then synthesized findings from the document reviews and informational discussions to identify potential actions that the U.S. Air Force could take to address constraints on ARC utilization. These include changes to statutes, resource and personnel management policies, and constraints to permeability—the ability of service members to transfer between the active and reserve components. Not all findings were selected to be incorporated into our recommendations; rather, we chose to focus on those findings that were dominant in our legal and policy reviews, as well as our discussions with senior U.S. Air Force leaders.

---

[11] This study received RAND Human Subject Protection Committee approval to proceed with informational discussions on October 9, 2017. We conducted discussions with 37 individuals during the course of the study.

Lastly, the study approach included an analysis of personnel data from the U.S. Air Force's Manpower Military Personnel Appropriations Man-Day Management System (M4S). The team analyzed data related to the demand for ARC support to operational missions, and the supply of ARC members filling that demand. This multifaceted approach allowed us to use various data sources and analyses to develop our recommendations to the U.S. Air Force.

Organization of This Report

Chapter Two examines the historical origins of the National Guard and Reserve, and its evolution from strategic reserve components to operational reserve components. Chapter Three examines the current utilization of the ARC. Chapter Four identifies current statutes that constrain utilization of ARC members for frequent or long-term active-duty missions. Chapter Five examines resource, policy and permeability issues that constrain utilization for ARC members for frequent or long-term active-duty missions. Chapter Six discusses our main conclusions from our findings and recommendations.

CHAPTER TWO

Historical Evolution from Strategic to Operational Reserve

Over time, the ARC has shifted from primarily a strategic force in the mid-twentieth century to today's operational force composed of both part-time and full-time members. Today, it is utilized to support humanitarian, peace-keeping, and military operations around the world; and key mission sets, including air sovereignty and remotely piloted aircraft, are carried out by ARC members. This chapter traces this evolution of the ARC from a strategic to an operational reserve.

Origins of the National Guard and Reserve

Since the country's inception, the U.S. military has had some form of reserve component. The reserve component stemmed from state militias, designed with the purpose of having able-bodied individuals with weapons available for muster when called to duty by the colonial, and eventually federal, government.[1] From about 1636 to 1903, state militias constituted the primary component of U.S. military forces, and except for during wartime, the federal government had less control over militias—largely because the country was still trying to clarify the roles and responsibilities of the federal government versus the states. Over time, the federal government grew increasingly concerned about the patchwork of uneven training, financing, and equipping across the state militias, as well as its inability to mobilize the militias

---

[1] Edward M. Goffman, "The Duality of the American Military Tradition: A Commentary," *Journal of Military History*, Vol. 64, No. 4, October 2000, p. 969.

quickly and effectively in response to a national threat. Toward the end of this era, the federal government took steps to gain increasing control over state militias.

The Dick Act of 1903 was a key piece of legislation because it was the first law to establish a relationship between the active and reserve components. It divided the militia into two groups: the "organized militia," defined as the regularly enlisted, organized, and uniformed active militia of the several states and territories; and the "reserve militia," consisting of all able-bodied male citizens ages 18–45. Organized militia units were subject to periodic inspection by active component officers, and the active component was required to provide the states with active army officers to train their militias.[2]

The Militia Act of 1908 further increased federal control over the militias by legally authorizing them to be called on for both domestic and foreign wars. It also required that state militias be mobilized before volunteer units could be formed in times of emergency, and it removed the traditional nine-month limitation on activation of the militia for federal service.[3]

The National Defense Act of 1916 continued this trend of federalization by mandating that the term *National Guard* be used instead of *militia*, providing for federal recognition of National Guard officers, and requiring that National Guard soldiers receive federal pay for drills.[4] The act also permitted the federal government to use the National Guard for overseas campaigns, building on the Militia Act of 1908.[5]

The National Defense Act of 1916 was also significant to the development of the ARC because it provided for a signal corps, which had an aviation section. This subsequently became the Army Air Corps, which Reserve officers supported. The National Security Act of 1947 officially designated

---

[2] Richard B. Crossland and James T. Currie, *Twice the Citizen: A History of the United States Army Reserve, 1908–1983*, Washington, D.C.: Office of the Chief, Army Reserve, 1984, p. 14.

[3] Crossland and Currie, 1984, p. 20.

[4] Michael D. Doubler, John W. Listman, and Donald M. Goldstein, *The National Guard: An Illustrated History of America's Citizens-Soldiers*, Dulles, Va.: Brassey's, 2003, p. 58.

[5] Doubler, Listman, and Goldstein, 2003, p. 393.

the ANG a reserve component of the U.S. Air Force.[6] The AFR was officially established as a reserve component of the U.S. Air Force on April 14, 1948, by a joint Department of the Army and Department of the Air Force directive, which ordered the transfer of all officers and enlisted individuals of the Air Corps Reserve to the AFR and abolished the Air Corps Reserve Section of the Army.[7]

The Use of the Reserve Components as a Strategic Reserve: World War I, World War II, Korea, and Vietnam

The National Defense Act of 1920 was instrumental in clearly articulating the relative roles of the active component and the reserve components by mandating that the Regular/Active Army and the Army National Guard serve as the nation's "first-line defense," with the Organized Reserve serving as the nation's "second-line defense."

From 1945 to 1989, reserve component members were rarely called on. They were involuntarily activated by the federal government only four times—an average of less than once per decade.[8] The reserve components were activated to augment active forces during World War I, World War II, and the Korean War.[9] However, while millions of U.S. service members eventually deployed to Vietnam, only 37,643 reserve component members (including all services) were involuntarily activated for service there.[10] By contrast, in 1969 alone, approximately 550,000 active component members

---

[6] Headquarters, United States Air Force, Office of Policy Integration, *2014 United Stated Air Force Reserve Handbook*, 2014, pp. 165–175; Public Law 80-253, National Security Act of 1947, July 26, 1947; and ANG, "History," webpage, undated.

[7] DA Cir. No. 103/DAF Letter 35-124, "Subj: Air Force Reserve and Air Force Honorary Retirees," April 14, 1948, MFA4002, AFRES.

[8] Kapp, 2010, p. 9.

[9] Office of the Vice Chairman of the Joint Chiefs of Staff and Office of the Assistant Secretary of Defense for Reserve Affairs, 2011, p. 15.

[10] Lawrence Kapp, *Involuntary Reserve Activations for U.S. Military Operations Since World War II*, Washington, D.C.: Congressional Research Service, 2000, p. 10.

served in Vietnam. In previous conflicts, the services had planned for substantial contributions from their reserve components. President Lyndon B. Johnson, however, elected not to mobilize the reserve components as the United States escalated its role in the Vietnam conflict in 1965. Both the civilian and uniformed leadership of DoD favored a partial mobilization of the reserve components to prosecute the Vietnam War, and they were shocked to learn of President Johnson's decision not to mobilize them.[11]

There is no indication that President Johnson failed to mobilize the reserve components for Vietnam because he believed they were ill prepared or unable to make a substantive contribution to the war. His decision not to mobilize them has instead been characterized as an "almost purely political decision."[12] A major reserve mobilization would have required scrutiny from Congress and the attention of the public, neither of which President Johnson wanted to risk.[13] An expert put it this way: "[President Johnson] tried to fight a war on the cheap and [he] tried to fight a war without acknowledging that he was fighting a war."[14] In sum, the decision not to utilize the reserve components in Vietnam was based on political calculation rather than military considerations.

The Emergence of Total Force Policy

As the U.S. government turned its attention and resources away from Southeast Asia and toward domestic concerns and confronting the Soviet Union in the aftermath of Vietnam, constrained fiscal resources weighed heavily on active-reserve force mix issues. From DoD's perspective, a more modest defense budget and the implementation of the All-Volunteer Force necessitated that the reserve components become a key contributor to national

---

[11] Lewis Sorley, "Reserve Components: Looking Back to Look Ahead," *Joint Forces Quarterly*, Vol. 36, 1st Quarter 2005, p. 19.

[12] James T. Currie and Richard B. Crossland, *Twice the Citizen: A History of the United States Army Reserve, 1908–1995*, Washington, D.C.: Department of the Army, 1997, p. 195.

[13] David Halberstam, *The Best and the Brightest*, New York: Random House, 1972.

[14] Lewis Sorley, "Creighton Abrams and Active-Reserve Integration in Wartime," *Parameters*, Vol. 21, Summer 1991, pp. 37–38.

security. The active component needed a major overhaul, even though defense budgets and personnel levels shrank dramatically. The reserve components offered an attractive solution to maintain sufficient war-making capability at a reduced cost. Thus, fiscal considerations were also a prime motivator in realigning the active-reserve force mix in the post-Vietnam era.

In 1970, then–Secretary of Defense Melvin Laird began to publicly champion a "total force concept" for the U.S. military. In a memorandum to the military services, Laird directed that "[a] total force concept will be applied in all aspects of planning, programming, manning, equipping and employing Guard and Reserve forces."[15] Laird's successor, James Schlesinger, formally adopted the concept as the "Total Force Policy" in 1973. In DoD's *Total Force Policy Report to Congress* in 1990, the Total Force Policy was described as having two principal tenets: "First, reliance on reserve forces as the primary augmentation for the active force; second, the integrated use of all forces that are available—active, reserve, civilian, and allied."[16]

According to DoD, much of the motivation for the Total Force Policy was budgetary rather than philosophical in nature.[17] Laird said in 1970, "Within the Department of Defense, economies will require reductions in over-all strengths and capabilities of the active forces, and increased reliance on the combat and combat support units of the Guard and Reserves."[18] He went on to describe how this new total force concept would have implications for the active-reserve force mix: "Emphasis will be given to the concurrent consideration of the Total Force, active and reserve, to determine the most advantageous mix to support national strategy and meet the threat."[19]

---

[15] Stephen M. Duncan, *Citizen Warriors: America's National Guard and Reserve Forces & the Politics of National Security*, Novato, Calif.: Presidio Press, 1997, p. 137.

[16] Office of the Secretary of Defense, Total Force Policy Group, *Total Force Policy Report to Congress*, Washington, D.C., December 31, 1990, p. 13.

[17] Richard W. Stewart, ed., *American Military History*, Volume II: *The United States Army in a Global Era, 1917–2003*, Washington, D.C.: Department of the Army, Center for Military History, 1989, p. 375.

[18] Duncan, 1997, p. 140.

[19] Duncan, 1997, p. 140.

At the same time, then–Army Chief of Staff General Creighton Abrams promoted the belief that the nation "must never go to war without the involvement of the Guard and Reserve and, thus, the support of the American people."[20] Abrams regarded the decision to not mobilize the reserve components for service in Vietnam as a critical error.[21]

The total force concept slowly gained support. It was first truly employed in 1990 during Operations Desert Shield and Desert Storm, where the United States mobilized approximately 238,729 reserve component members.[22] During these conflicts, the U.S. Air Force activated approximately 36,000 ARC members (23,500 AFR and 12,400 ANG).[23] President George Bush said of the triumph, "This victory belongs . . . to the Regulars, to the Reserves, to the National Guard."[24]

The Evolution of the Air Reserve Component into an Operational Reserve

The ARC's evolution from a strategic reserve component to an operational reserve component was prompted primarily by shifts in the strategic environment. The aftermath of 9/11 led to an increase in the demand for U.S. military forces to project U.S. power around the globe and the emergence of the ARC as an operational force. Department of Defense Directive 1200.17 defines *operational force* as follows:

> RCs as an operational force. The RCs provide operational capabilities and strategic depth to meet U.S. defense requirements across the

---

[20] Office of the Vice Chairman of the Joint Chiefs of Staff and Office of the Assistant Secretary of Defense for Reserve Affairs, 2011, p. 15.

[21] Sorley, 2005, p. 22.

[22] Kapp, 2000, pp. 13–14.

[23] Air Reserve Personnel Center, "A Look Back at Desert Storm," HQ Air Force Reserve Command Public Affairs, January 14, 2016; National Guard, "25th Anniversary: Operation Desert Storm," webpage, 2016.

[24] Michael D. Doubler, *Civilian in Peace, Soldier in War: The Army National Guard, 1636–2000*, Lawrence, Kan.: University Press of Kansas, 2003, p. 301.

full spectrum of conflict. In their operational roles, RCs participate in a full range of missions according to their services' force generation plans. Units and individuals participate in missions in an established cyclic or periodic manner that provides predictability for the combatant commands (CCMDs), the services, service members, their families, and employers. In their strategic roles, RC units and individuals train or are available for missions in accordance with the national defense strategy. As such, the RCs provide strategic depth and are available to transition to operational roles as needed.[25]

Despite these changes, the operational force continues to contain elements of a strategic force. In a 2013 memorandum, the Office of the Secretary of Defense's Reserve Forces Policy Board (RFPB) offered the following definition of an operational reserve:

> Routine, recurring utilization of the reserve components as a fully integrated part of the operational force that is planned and programmed by the services. As such, the "Operational Reserve" is that reserve component structure which is made ready and available to operate across the continuum of military missions, performing strategic and operational roles, in peacetime, in wartime and in support of civil authorities. The services organize, man, train, equip, resource and use their reserve components to support mission requirements following the same standards as their active components.[26]

This definition highlights the fact that the reserve components have both a strategic role and an operational role under the operational force construct. In their strategic role, which includes the capability to transition to the operational role, the reserve components direct units and individuals to train and be available for missions in accordance with the national defense strategy. In

---

[25] Department of Defense Directive 1200.17, *Managing the Reserve Components as an Operational Force*, October 29, 2008, p. 8.

[26] Reserve Forces Policy Board (RFPB), Information Memo from MajGen Arnold Panuro, USMCR (Ret), Chairman, Reserve Policy Board, "Report of the Reserve Forces Policy Board on the 'Operational Reserve' and Inclusion of the Reserve Components in Key Department of Defense (DoD) Processes," January 14, 2013, pp. 1–2.

their operational roles, the reserve components participate in a full range of operational missions. Yet there is inherent tension and contradiction in the operational force construct, for it insists on having reserve components—which are, by definition, a part-time force to be held in "reserve"—that are also ready for conflict at any time.

CHAPTER THREE

How the Air Reserve Component Is Currently Utilized for Frequent and Long-Term Active-Duty Missions

Introduction

ARC personnel are utilized to perform frequent or long-term active component operational requirements. Data on the demand for ARC personnel provide insight into which Air Force Specialty Codes (AFSCs), skill sets, ranks, and mission sets the active component cannot fill on its own.

Another way to identify where the active component cannot meet demand is by analyzing the number of heavily utilized ARC personnel. Members of the AFR and ANG are protected from overutilization by statutes, personnel policies, and resource policies. One requirement is that a member who serves on active duty or FTNG providing operational support for more than 1,095 man-days out of the previous 1,460 days must be counted in active-duty (or AGR) end strength. This is commonly referred to as the "1,095 man-day rule," which was enacted in 2004 to address the many concerns expressed about the prior-strength accounting limitation. The prior provision required a reserve component member on active duty for special work for more than 180 days to be accounted for in the active-duty end-strength authorization. The 1,095 man-day rule allows reserve component members to remain on duty to complete a requirement or mission for up to three years without interruption or a break in pay and benefits. Tracking the number of ARC members who exceed the 1,095 man-day rule can help identify high-demand AFSCs, ranks, mission sets, and individuals used to fill active component missions.

This chapter provides analysis of the demand for ARC personnel by requested AFSC (enlisted and officer), level of support, mission area, requirement category, and mission region. We then provide a characterization of individuals approaching the 1,095 man-day rule reporting requirement by rank, ARC status, and unit type. Analysis of ARC individuals approaching the requirement offers insights into where the active component has become reliant on ARC personnel, and an opportunity to examine the current force mix.

Data Sources

This study accessed three main data sets within the M4S through the U.S. Air Force: the Beast table, the Mobilization on Tour (MOT) table, and the Active-Duty Operational Support (ADOS) table. The Beast table contains all the requests for man-days in FY 2018, including the requester, justification, impact if not funded, and number of days approved. The MOT table contains information regarding the individuals filling the man-day requirement. The ADOS table contains information about individuals approaching the reporting requirement under the 1,095 man-day rule. In combination, the data provided allow for a fuller understanding of both the demand for and supply of ARC individuals.

Air Reserve Component Requests

The following section characterizes requests for ARC individuals. Such characteristics include requested AFSCs (for both enlisted airmen and officers) and requests by type of support, level of support, mission area, requirement category, and mission region.

Requested Air Reserve Component Air Force Specialty Codes

Tables 3.1 and 3.2 present man-day requests for the ten most requested AFSCs in descending order of the number of requests made in FY 2018.

TABLE 3.1

Ten Most Requested Enlisted Air Force Specialty Codes for Air Reserve Component Missions, Fiscal Year 2018

AFSC	AFSC Title	Days Requested	Days Approved	Request Count
1N0XX	Operations Intelligence	368,914	57,441	220
3D0XX	Knowledge Operations Management	165,891	58,601	211
3S0XX	Personnel	94,129	27,938	178
3D1XX	Client Systems	248,489	78,967	168
3P0XX	Security Forces	169,346	82,624	150
2A5XX	Aerospace Maintenance	336,573	69,398	110
1N4XX	Network Intelligence Analyst	112,781	38,163	96
1N1XX	Geospatial Intelligence	177,587	48,335	93
4N0XX	Aerospace Medical Service	86,512	38,180	92
3A1XX	Information Management	31,503	11,838	91
Total, 10 most requested AFSCs		1,791,725	511,485	1,409
Total, all requested AFSCs	112 AFSCs	12,086,659	3,561,446	3,556

SOURCE: Beast Table in M4S data set.

Requests can be quantified through two metrics. The "request count" variable captures the number of individual requests made by unit for ARC service members by AFSC. It is important to note that the request count does not capture individual billets but instead measures the number of times units made a request for ARC service members. A high request count indicates that individual units discovered more demand than they were capable of filling internally. The "days requested" variable captures the stated demand for man-days by AFSC, while the "days approved" variable

TABLE 3.2

Ten Most Requested Officer Air Force Specialty Codes for Air Reserve Component Missions, Fiscal Year 2018

AFSC	AFSC Title	Days Requested	Days Approved	Request Count
14N	Intelligence	270,716	48,115	444
11M	Mobility Pilot	368,361	114,780	237
17D	Cyberspace Operations Commander	79,044	28,852	233
16G	Air Force Operations Staff Officer	79,424	27,916	228
11F	Fighter Pilot	537,390	112,814	196
62E	Developmental Engineer	13,152	6,766	133
16R	Planning and Programming	30,955	14,706	121
32E	Civil Engineer	23,929	7,445	119
38P	Personnel Officer	38,601	15,713	113
90G	General Officer	18,542	8,825	113
Total, 10 most requested AFSCs		1,460,114	385,932	1,937
Total, all requested AFSCs	107 AFSCs	3,571,013	1,098,815	4,195

SOURCE: Beast table in M4S data set.

captures the number of days approved for ARC positions from the given AFSC.[1] (For a more comprehensive list of all man-day requests by AFSC, see Appendix A.)

---

[1] Air Force Instruction (AFI) 36-2619 and AFI 10-301 define the criteria used for man-day approvals. The U.S. Air Force uses a requirements-based process to "identify and validate all Man-Day requirements," validated through senior U.S. Air Force leadership "for approval and linked to resource allocation decisions." The U.S. Air Force operations directorate manages ARC operational utilization requirements by "collecting, categorizing and prioritizing operational mission requirements with cross-functional coordination at all levels." The directorate collects ARC operational utilization requirements and prioritizes the requirements using a weighted methodology. Air Force Instruction 36-2619, *Military Personnel Appropriation Man-Day Program*, July 18, 2014, p. 17.

Among enlisted airmen, Operations Intelligence service members were in highest demand. Units were approved for 57,441 man-days of Operations Intelligence ARC support.

Of the 107 officer AFSCs captured in Table A.1, 5 AFSCs represent over 30 percent of all requests: intelligence officers, mobility pilots, cyberspace operations commanders, U.S. Air Force operations staff officers, and fighter pilots (n = 1,338 out of the total 4,195). Pilots are in highest demand; requests for mobility pilots and fighter pilots combined account for 905,751 man-day requests and 227,594 approved man-days in the ARC. The highest nonpilot demand is for intelligence officers, totaling 270,716 requested man-days and 48,115 approved man-days.

Air Reserve Component Requests by Unit Type of Support

The largest number of requests for ARC individuals is on headquarters staffs, and the largest numbers of days requested are from combat units, followed by combat support and combat service support units (Table 3.3). However, combat service support accounts for the largest number of approved man-days (over 3 million). Combat service support includes administrative roles (finance, resource management), medical support, and legal support,

TABLE 3.3

Air Reserve Component Requests by Type of Support, Fiscal Year 2018

Type of Support	Days Requested	Days Approved	Request Count
Combat	5,664,468	691,037	385
Combat service support	4,483,957	3,112,887	2,326
Combat support	4,558,979	627,863	1,935
Headquarters staff	788,343	283,923	2,839
Unknown	150,503	8,235	167
Total	15,646,250	4,723,945	7,652

SOURCE: Beast table in M4S data set.

NOTE: The total reflects data variation by type of support, command level, mission area, and requirement category as reported in the M4S data set.

among others. By utilizing the ARC for support functions, the active component may be able to reallocate its end strength to combat roles.

Air Reserve Component Requests by Command Level

The majority of individual requests and approved man-days were apportioned to operational units (wings, groups, and squadrons) in FY 2018
(Table 3.4). CCMDs and Major Commands account for another 33 percent
of ARC requests. The large number of days requested indicates that the
active component has shortfalls that must be supplemented by the ARC.

Air Reserve Component Requests by Mission Area

The largest number of requests in FY 2018 were apportioned to management headquarters (Table 3.5). However, the largest number of man-days

TABLE 3.4

**Air Reserve Component Requests by Command Level,
Fiscal Year 2018**

Type of Support	Days Requested	Days Approved	Request Count
Air Force level	285,409	123,283	852
CCMD	2,482,228	319,100	857
Defense agency	22,221	6,547	99
Joint staff	18,104	6,086	58
Major Command or numbered Air Force	596,014	313,010	1,662
Operational (wing/group/ squadron)	12,176,403	3,955,919	4,075
Reimbursable	2,695	0	5
Unknown	80	0	1
Total	15,583,154	4,723,945	7,609

SOURCE: Beast table in M4S data set.

NOTE: The total reflects data variation by type of support, command level, mission area, and
requirement category as reported in the M4S data set.

22

TABLE 3.5

Air Reserve Component Requests by Mission Area, Fiscal Year 2018

Mission Area	Days Requested	Days Approved	Request Count
Management headquarters	438,769	163,302	1,501
Personnel and training	745,995	386,301	769
Mobility	2,253,551	429,786	662
Intelligence, surveillance, and reconnaissance	1,447,526	428,099	489
Special Operations Forces (SOF)	124,494	91,458	412
Attack	6,008,125	2,447,424	351
Research, development, testing, and evaluation	57,892	14,648	347
Cyber	249,453	74,051	346
Command and Control	280,033	98,833	328
National Intelligence Program	95,927	16,843	232
Air superiority	410,938	241,307	200
Logistics	69,698	11,870	197
Space	131,220	28,350	195
Nuclear operations	74,299	21,442	187
N/A	1,602,717	0	166
Bomber	40,631	21,132	61
Personnel recovery	124,032	34,908	57
Search and rescue	4,014	2,622	23
Communication infrastructure	3,250	2,520	6
National Intelligence Program–outside Air Force	2,190	731	3
Installations	2,567	0	2
Special operations forces–outside Air Force	10,712	5,767	2
Total	14,178,033	4,521,394	6,536

SOURCE: Beast table in M4S data set.

NOTE: The "N/A" category includes ARC requests with incomplete mission area data. The total reflects data variation by type of support, command level, mission area, and requirement category as reported in the M4S data set.

was apportioned to attack units, followed by mobility and intelligence, surveillance, and reconnaissance units. Notably, the highest numbers of days approved are in operational mission areas (e.g., attack; mobility; intelligence, surveillance, and reconnaissance; air superiority).

Air Reserve Component Requests by Requirement Category

Overwhelmingly, ARC individuals supported new missions, with more than 2 million approved man-days (Table 3.6). A new mission is defined as one

TABLE 3.6

Air Reserve Component Requests by Requirement Category, Fiscal Year 2018

Mission Area	Days Requested	Days Approved	Request Count
New mission	5,287,994	2,157,295	1,280
Emergent requirement	193,502	−339	717
Manning augmentation	458,285	9,036	528
Previous Program Objective Memorandum (POM) requirement	3,324,103	494,014	513
Emergent requirement— mission critical	335,347	11,680	247
Increase baseline	79,361	52,482	76
Special project	36,344	365	75
Mission adjustment	8,816	6,250	30
Mission transfer	12,410	0	13
Exception to policy	1,100	0	3
Total	9,737,262	2,731,461	3,482

SOURCE: Beast table in M4S data set.

NOTES: Policy defines requirement categories as either "enduring" or "emergent." The M4S data set separates requirement categories further into the ten categories listed in this table. The M4S data dictionary did not provide a definition for the difference between a "new mission" and "emergent requirement." The total reflects data variation by type of support, command level, mission area, and requirement category as reported in the M4S data set. The negative approval figure for emergent requirements represents a budget adjustment.

in which a requirement did not exist in the previous fiscal year. The largest number of days requested was also for new missions, indicating a shortfall in the active component. The use of ARC individuals for new missions highlights the critical role the ARC plays, ensuring that the active component is able to meet unforeseen demand.

Air Reserve Component Requests by Mission Region

As shown in Table 3.7, most ARC individuals served in the continental United States in day-to-day operations (with a day-to-day operations tour count of 42,244). Those serving in active contingency operations were most likely to support missions in the Central Command Area of Responsibility (Iraq and Afghanistan).

TABLE 3.7

Air Reserve Component Requests by Mission Region/ Combatant Command, Fiscal Year 2018

Region	Day-to-Day Operations (tour count)	Overseas Contingency Operations (OCO) Tour Count
Continental United States	42,244	16,273
Africa Command	15	157
Central Command Area of Responsibility	451	17,482
European Command	596	22
Northern Command	335	15
Indo-Pacific Command	1,063	30
Southern Command	296	8
Total	44,704	33,987

SOURCE: MOT table in M4S data set.

Man-Days Served by Individuals over the 1,095 Man-Day Rule

An examination of the number and types of individuals approaching the 1,095 man-day rule may provide insights into where the active component may not be meeting sustained demand. This section examines three characteristics of individuals approaching the 1,095 man-day rule in FY 2018: rank, ARC status, and unit type.

Man-Days Served by Individuals over the 1,095 Man-Day Rule by Rank

Of those individuals serving over the 1,095 man-day rule, among officers, O-5s (lieutenant colonels) served the most man-days past the threshold by a total of 8,301 man-days (Table 3.8). At the general-officer level, only O-8s

TABLE 3.8

Number of Man-Days Served over the 1,095 Man-Day Threshold by Rank, Fiscal Year 2018

Rank	Number of Man-Days
Officer	
O1	42
O2	136
O3	1,217
O4	5,066
O5	8,301
O6	2,942
O7	0
O8	366
O9	0
O10	0
Total officer	**18,070**

Table 3.8—Continued

Rank	Number of Man-Days
Enlisted	
E1	178
E2	1,407
E3	4,331
E4	4,920
E5	5,175
E6	1,833
E7	566
E8	0
E9	0
Total enlisted	**18,410**
Total officer and enlisted	**36,480**

SOURCE: ADOS table in M4S data set.

(major generals) served in the ARC past the threshold, by a total of 366 man-days. Among enlisted service members, E-5s represented the largest number of man-days served past the threshold (5,175 man-days). Individuals in the junior enlisted ranks of E-1 and E-2 served a total of 1,585 days over the 1,095 man-day threshold.

Individuals Exceeding the 1,095 Man-Day Rule by Air Reserve Component Status

TRs and DSGs represent the highest numbers of individuals approaching the 1,095 man-day rule (1,700 combined; Table 3.9). Reserve IMAs represent the next-highest proportion of service members approaching the rule.

TABLE 3.9

Individuals Approaching 1,095 Man-Day Rule by Personnel Category, FY 2018

Personnel Category	Number of Individuals
AFR: IMA	564
AFR: TR	773
ANG: DSG	927
Total	2,264

SOURCE: ADOS table in M4S data set.

Man-Days Served by Individuals Exceeding the 1,095 Man-Day Rule by Unit/Organization Type

In FY 2018, individuals over the 1,095 man-day threshold served for a total of 40,205 man-days (Table 3.10). Many of these man-days (11,525) were utilized by Readiness and Integration Organizations, which include CCMD staffs and Major Command staffs.[2] However, operational units including wings, groups, and squadrons together accounted for the majority (71.3 percent)[3] of all man-days served by individuals serving in the ARC for more than 1,095 man-days. Fighter wings, bomber wings, airlift wings, air refueling wings, and intelligence wings accounted for over one-half of all man-days served by individuals over the 1,095 man-day threshold, indicating a high demand for (and potential low supply of) individuals able to fill those units.

---

[2] Readiness and Integration Organizations serve to "seamlessly integrate war-time ready Individual Reserve Forces to meet Air Force and Combatant Commander Requirements" and manage IMA end strength. Headquarters Individual Reservist Readiness Integration Organization, "About HQ Rio."

[3] Calculated as the proportion of all non–Readiness and Integration Organization detachment unit assignment man-days divided by the total number of all unit assignment man-days.

TABLE 3.10

Number of Man-Days Served over the 1,095 Man-Day Threshold by Unit/Organization Type, Fiscal Year 2018

Type of Unit/Organization	Total Number of Man-Days over 1,095
Readiness and Integration Organization detachments	11,525
Fighter	6,767
Bomber	6,462
Air refueling	2,940
Airlift	2,915
Intelligence	2,265
Reserve support	1,812
Wing (unspecified)	1,609
Special operations	1,173
Rescue	500
Reconnaissance	381
Regional support	366
Attack	314
Combat operations support	274
Air mobility	272
Training	219
Space	136
Air control	120
Air operations	99
Civil engineer	56
Total	40,205

SOURCE: ADOS table in M4S data set.

NOTE: Discrepancies between the total by unit/organizational type and the total presented in Table 3.8 are reflective of variations in the original data presented in the ADOS table.

Conclusion

The ARC is a crucial enabler for the active component's meeting demand. The ARC allows the total U.S. Air Force to ensure the nation's security, providing agile and adaptive capacity to fulfill existing, new, and emergent missions. However, the long-term use of ARC individuals, particularly those approaching or requiring 1,095 man-day waivers, indicates that positions exist where the active component may be unable to meet demand—even with the ability to plan against the demand for three or more years. Therefore, the roles, ranks, types of missions, level of assignments, and areas of assignment provide insights as to where the active component may have shortfalls. The trends may also reflect preferences among ARC members seeking to prolong their active-duty utilization. The trends reflected in RegAF demand for ARC personnel mirror the AFSCs and ranks where the RegAF currently faces retention difficulties. Pilots and maintainers represent the highest RegAF demand, followed by intelligence officers and noncommissioned officers. Midcareer officers and enlisted personnel represent the plurality of demand.

CHAPTER FOUR

Statutory Constraints to Utilization of Air Reserve Component Members

In the face of evolving security threats, the relationship between full-time active-duty forces of the U.S. Air Force and the ARC has changed over time. Confronted with the declining size of the active-duty force and reduced budgets, the U.S. Air Force reexamined its management of the total U.S. Air Force following the first Persian Gulf War, when the military was experiencing a significant drawdown of both active and reserve forces. Recently, consensus has emerged among policymakers, think tanks, and other thought leaders that the U.S. Air Force would benefit from a closer operational relationship between the ARC and RegAF.[1]

Congress mandated the creation of the National Commission on the Structure of the Air Force (NCSAF) under the auspices of the Fiscal Year 2013 National Defense Authorization Act, to "determine whether, and how, the structure should be modified to best fulfill current and anticipated mission requirements . . . in a manner consistent with available resources."[2] The commission released a report of its findings in 2014, with a key recommendation that called for the U.S. Air Force to "entrust as many missions as possible to its reserve component forces."[3]

---

[1] NCSAF, *Report to the President and Congress of the United States*, Arlington, Va., January 30, 2014, p. 1.

[2] Public Law 112-239, National Defense Authorization Act for Fiscal Year 2013, January 2, 2013.

[3] NCSAF, 2014, p. 7.

A 2014 RAND report also examined issues that have affected the suitability of missions for assignment to reserve component forces.[4] Most notably, the report highlighted the statutory and funding challenges imposed by increased use of the ARC for active missions. Since the release of the report, the RFPB came to similar findings in a 2016 report, which concluded that "outdated personnel management policies, statutes, and information systems create inefficiencies that reduce the services' desire to use the reserve components and negatively impacts the overall effectiveness of the Total Force."[5]

This chapter will provide an overview of the legal structure for governing utilization of the ARC and associated funding, and how those provisions of law affect ARC support for active-duty missions. Most notably, this chapter will focus on statutes that provide for ordering an ANG or AFR member to perform duty, whether for training, operational support, staff or administrative functions, or various other purposes such as receiving health care or becoming the subject of disciplinary proceedings. This chapter will also describe the constraints that affect the utilization of the ARC force to conduct sustained active-duty missions. The following are the four major constraints to utilization of the reserve components: (1) the duty status system; (2) the legal structure, which dictates rigid funding streams for components; (3) the current 1,095 man-day strength accounting requirement, which potentially constrains volunteerism; and (4) the limitations on duties that FTS personnel may perform.

Our findings presented in this chapter are consistent with the findings of previous studies and the Office of the Air Force Judge Advocate General regarding the legal challenges and barriers that affect the utilization of ARC forces to support operational missions.

---

[4] Albert A. Robbert, James H. Bigelow, John E. Boon, Jr., Lisa M. Harrington, Michael McGee, S. Craig Moore, Daniel M. Norton, and William W. Taylor, *Suitability of Missions for the Air Force*, Santa Monica, CA: RAND Corporation, RR-429-AF, 2014.

[5] RFPB, *Improving the Total Force: Using the National Guard and Reserves*, Falls Church, Va.: Office of the Secretary of Defense, November 2016, p. 13.

Legal Structure for Employing Reserve Component Forces

This section describes the legal structure that is the foundation for employing reserve component forces, which begins with the pertinent articles of the U.S. Constitution. We then focus on the authorities to order a reserve component member to perform duty and the limitations those authorities impose. Finally, we characterize legal constraints on the appropriation of funds for utilizing reserve component forces, focusing on how appropriated funds may be used and the consequences of misusing those funds.

Key Constitutional Provisions

At the root of the legal restrictions for employing reserve component members to support active-duty missions is the republican and tripartite nature of the U.S. government (executive, legislative, and judiciary), as outlined in the Constitution. As stated in Articles I and II of the Constitution, the legislative and executive branches have specific powers related to governing the military as a whole.

Under Article I, Congress shall provide for the "common defence."[6] To do so, it is given the authority to raise and support armies, provide and maintain a navy, and declare war.[7] The Constitution also prescribes certain powers specifically related to the militia, which developed into today's National Guard. Specifically, Congress has the power to "provide for organizing, arming, and disciplining, the Militia, and for governing such Part of them as may be employed in the Service of the United States, reserving to the States respectively, . . . the Authority of training the Militia according to the discipline prescribed by Congress,"[8] and of "calling forth the Militia to execute the Laws of the Union, suppress Insurrections and repel invasions."[9]

---

[6] U.S. Constitution, Article I, Section 8, Clause 1.

[7] U.S. Constitution, Article I, Section 8, Clauses 11, 12, 13.

[8] U.S. Constitution, Article I, Section 8, Clause 16.

[9] U.S. Constitution, Article I, Section 8, Clause 15.

The Constitution carefully distinguishes between federal and state control of the National Guard. The president is the commander in chief of the National Guard, but only when called into federal service. At all other times, the role of commander in chief of the National Guard resides with the governor of each state with respect to the National Guard of that state. In the case of the District of Columbia, which does not have a governor, that role is filled by the District of Columbia National Guard's commanding general.

Finally, regarding the executive branch, Article II prescribes that the "President shall be the Commander-in-Chief of the Army and Navy of the United States and of the Militia of the several States, when called into the actual Service of the United States."[10]

Title 10 of the U.S. Code

Title 10 of the U.S.C. plays a major role in this discussion, since most of the duty statuses are prescribed in that title. Underlying the authorities to order a reserve component member to perform duty, Title 10 also prescribes the purpose of the reserve components:

> to provide trained units and qualified persons available for active duty in the armed forces, in time of war or national emergency, and at such other times as the national security may require, to fill the needs of the armed forces whenever more units and persons are needed than are in the regular components.[11]

It is worth noting that in 2004, this provision of Title 10 was amended by striking the phrase "during and after the period needed to procure and train additional units and qualified persons to achieve the planned mobilization."[12] Striking this phrase provides greater flexibility to employ the reserve components as an operational force, rather than simply as a strategic reserve to be activated when needed for mobilization. Thus, Title 10 now provides for an operational reserve.

---

[10] U.S. Constitution, Article II, Section 2, Clause 1.

[11] 10 U.S.C. § 10102.

[12] Public Law 108-375, Ronald W. Reagan National Defense Authorization Act for Fiscal Year 2005, Section 511, October 28, 2004, 118 Stat. 1877.

Title 10 also describes the basic policy for ordering the reserve components to active duty:

> Whenever Congress determines that more units and organizations are needed for the national security than are in the regular components of the ground and air forces, the Army National Guard of the United States and the Air National Guard of the United States . . . together with units of other reserve components necessary for a balanced force, shall be ordered to active duty and retained as long as so needed.[13]

Title 32 of the U.S. Code

Title 32 contains a similar policy for the Army National Guard and the ANG. The second sentence of that policy statement contains language that is almost identical to that found in Title 10:

> Whenever Congress determines that more units and organizations are needed for the national security than are in the regular components of the ground and air forces . . . the Air National Guard of the United States . . . together with such units of other reserve components as are necessary for a balanced force, shall be ordered to active Federal duty and retained as long as so needed.[14]

In addition to federal service under Title 10, Title 32 provides the authority for the governor of a state, the Commonwealth of Puerto Rico, Guam, or the Virgin Islands—or, in the case of the District of Columbia's National Guard, the commanding general—to order members of the National Guard to duty for training as provided in the Constitution. As the role of the National Guard has evolved, provisions have been enacted in Title 32 that provide authority for the National Guard to carry out a limited number of operational support activities that are federally funded but with command and control remaining with the governor. FTNG duty, which is performed under Title 32, is the general equivalent of active duty and accounts for 4 of the 27 duty statuses, in that it is federally funded, but with command and

---

[13] 10 U.S.C. § 10103.

[14] 32 U.S.C. § 102.

control resting with the governor (or the commanding general, in the case of the District of Columbia's National Guard), rather than the president of the United States.

Reserve Component Duty Status System

One of the biggest challenges of utilizing reserve component forces to support active-duty missions is the reserve component duty status system. This system determines the conditions under which a reserve component member can be ordered to perform duty and any requirements or restrictions associated with that duty. The number of reserve component duty statutes identified in various studies over the last 16 years varies from 29 to 32.[15] The numbers vary because different studies have used different criteria for counting the number of duty statuses, and additional duty statutes have been added over time. The lower range reflects only duty statutes authorized in law, while the higher number includes duty statutes authorized in both law and policy. DoD has recently identified 27 provisions of law that provide for ordering a reserve component member to perform military duty.[16] Regardless of the exact number, virtually every study of the reserve duty system has identified the complexity of the reserve duty status system as a problem that must be addressed.

The current reserve component duty status construct is based on maintaining a Cold War–era strategic reserve. Previously, reserve component members would train and be available in time of war or national emergency.[17] After training or being released from a mobilization, the member would

---

[15] Wexford Group International, *Reserve Component Military Duty Status Study: Considerations on Changing the Reserve Component Duty Status System (Phase II, Task 1)*, May 31, 2002, p. ii. Also see DoD, *Report of the Eleventh Quadrennial Review of Military Compensation: Main Report*, Washington, D.C., June 2012, p. 134; DoD, *Report of the Military Compensation and Retirement Modernization Commission: Final Report*, January 2015, p. 4; NCSAF, 2014, p. 25; and RFPB, 2016.

[16] DoDI 1215.06, 2014, Appendix to Enclosure 4, p. 22.

[17] Michelle Dolfini-Reed and Darlene E. Stafford, *Identifying Duty Status Reforms Needed to Support an Operational Reserve*, Alexandria, Va.: Center for Naval Analyses, CRM D0021656.A2, 2010, p. 15.

return to his or her civilian endeavors. Training and mobilization were intended to be separate and distinct, never intertwined.[18]

Use of today's reserve components is quite different, as reserve component members often shift from one duty status to another in support of ongoing operational missions. This new use of the reserve components has highlighted the dysfunction created by the current system.

Various provisions of law play a role in controlling the type and periods of duty a reserve component member may perform. As previously noted, Congress has enacted 27 different provisions of law under which reserve component members can be called or ordered to duty. Most of these statutes specifically state the purpose of the duty and might impose restrictions on the use of that particular duty authority. Further, when the purpose of the duty changes—for example, from performing an operational mission to receiving medical care for an injury sustained during the mission—a new order must be issued to comply with the purpose of the duty.

Voluntary and Involuntary Duty Distinctions

Duty statuses can further be broken into voluntary and involuntary duty. The statutes that provide for the activation of reserve component members, without the consent of the member, impose certain restrictions, while voluntary duty authorities themselves generally impose no constraints[19]— although other provisions of law, such as strength accounting, can impose certain requirements. Voluntary duty for reserve component members with a federal status is provided for under 10 U.S.C. § 12301(d); and voluntary FTNG duty, under which the member does not have a federal status, is provided for under 32 U.S.C. § 502(f)(1)(B).

A member performing voluntary duty under Title 10 may be deployed worldwide for training or operational missions. Because a member of the National Guard performing duty under Title 32 is under the command and control of the respective governor, or commanding general in the case of

---

[18] DoD, 2015, p. 53.

[19] 10 U.S.C. § 12301(d) does specify that a member of the Army National Guard of the United States or the ANG of the United States may not be ordered to active duty under this subsection without the consent of the governor or other appropriate authority of the state concerned.

the District of Columbia's National Guard, that duty authority should not be used to order a member of the Army National Guard or ANG to perform duty when command and control must be exercised by the president of the United States. This is because that duty will be performed in a region that is beyond the jurisdiction of the governor of the state.

Involuntary duty authorities for operational missions are performed under sections of law that are shown in Table 4.1.

The Title 10 provisions state the purposes for which the member may be called or ordered to duty under each provision of law, restrict who may be called up, and can restrict how many members can be on duty at any one time and how long a member may serve under that call-up authority. In contrast, the Title 32 provision simply provides the authority to order a member of the National Guard to FTNG duty without the consent of the member. Unlike the Title 10 provisions, there are no restrictions on the duration or number of members who can be ordered to FTNG duty under this authority, although some other provisions of Title 32 for which this authority is used do place restrictions on the duration of the duty.

TABLE 4.1

Authorities to Involuntarily Order a Reserve Component Member to Duty for Operational Missions

Section of the U.S.C.	Purpose
10 U.S.C. § 251	Insurrection
10 U.S.C. § 252	Enforce federal authority
10 U.S.C. § 12301(a)	War or national emergency declared by Congress: full mobilization
10 U.S.C. § 12302	National emergency declared by the President: partial mobilization
10 U.S.C. § 12304	Other than war or national emergency: presidential reserve call-up
10 U.S.C. § 12304a	Respond to a major disaster or emergency
10 U.S.C. § 12304b	Support to combatant commanders for preplanned missions
10 U.S.C. § 12406	National Guard called into federal service: insurrection
32 U.S.C. § 502(f)(1)(A)	Support missions: homeland defense activities; requests from the President or Secretary of Defense

Transitions Between Active-Duty and Full-Time National Guard Duty

The transition from FTNG duty to active duty, or active duty to FTNG duty, can be time consuming and disrupt pay and benefits. This occurs when a National Guard member is on FTNG duty to prepare for an activation and then is activated under Title 10. The same problems can be encountered when a National Guard member returns from an activation and transitions to FTNG duty, for example, to complete reintegration activities. The distinction between performing duty under different titles, as described in the previous section, may appear arbitrary when active component and National Guard members are serving side by side to support the same mission, but it requires a National Guard member to transition from duty under Title 32 to duty under Title 10. Simply stated, when National Guard members deploy overseas, they are performing a federal mission. Under Title 10, command and control transfers to the president in his role as the commander-in-chief of the armed forces, rather than remaining with the governor, even if the members are performing the same duties overseas as they were training for with their National Guard units in the United States. National Guard members do train to the same standards as active members, so it is not unusual for them to be working side by side performing the same job. To the National Guard member, this makes the transition to Title 10 seem unnecessary. Many interviewees highlighted the frustration with these distinctions, with one telling us,

> I believe the reason we put folks on Title 10 in theater is because of benefits, Status of Forces agreement, and line of duty determinations. Otherwise, tell me how a KC-135 maintainer's job is different in Kuwait than back home in Kansas when he's in a Title 32 status? The truth is, we put people in Title 10 for the benefits in case someone were to lob a shell onto a flight line or something of the sort.[20]

The same interviewee noted that transitioning between Title 10 and Title 32 can cause confusion and delay over pay. Placing someone on Military Personnel Appropriations (MPA) man-days can delay pay for weeks

---

[20] Interview AF7, ANG official, November 7, 2017.

or even months,[21] so units choose to keep members under Title 32 orders if they can; however, according to the interviewees, "if you keep doing this, it adds up for the Guard."[22]

While this may be the perceived reason for the transition, there are actually very few differences between the pay and benefits provided for duty under Title 10 and those provided under Title 32. Moreover, there is a provision of law in Title 10 that specifies that for the purposes of laws providing benefits for members of the National Guard and their dependents, duty under Title 32 shall be treated as federal service under Title 10.[23] There are additional pay and benefits provided to members who serve in a combat zone or hostile fire area, which are typically overseas, making it appear that duty performed under Title 10 provides additional pay and benefits beyond those for duty performed under Title 32. As previously described, compensation is not the reason National Guard members are placed under federal control when deployed outside the United States; it is ultimately about who is in charge of federal missions, the president or a governor.

It is important to note that while there may be few differences between the pay and benefits provided for duty under Title 10 and those provided under Title 32, the disruptions in pay and benefits that result from transitioning between different duty statuses are a critical complaint that we heard about repeatedly in our interviews. As several individuals told us,

---

[21] MPA days are used to support the active component missions. AFI 36-2619 outlines the process of putting ARC members on MPA man-days: "The Air Force Directorate for Manpower, Organization and Resources (AF/A1M) determines the eligible amount of man-days that may be applied to each valid Active Duty for Operational Support-Active Component requirement using manpower programming guidance issued at the beginning of the POM cycle. AF/A1M also provides eligible amounts of man-days for each command to the Air Force Directorate of Operations, War Planning and Policy Division (AF/A3OD)." The Major Commands collect man-day requirements from subordinate commands, prioritize those requests, and send them to the Assistant Secretary of the Air Force for Manpower and Reserve Affairs (SAF/MR).

[22] Interview AF3, senior U.S. Air Force officers, April 26, 2018.

[23] 10 U.S.C. § 12602.

these disruptions happen so often that they make it "too hard to serve."[24] Another asked, "Why is it so hard to get my paycheck?"[25]

Legal Constraints on Appropriated Funds for Utilizing Air Reserve Component Members

Title 31 U.S.C. Section 1301(a), also known as the Purpose Statute, requires that appropriated funds be spent only for the reasons prescribed for the funding. There are distinct funding streams that finance the operations of the active component, Reserves, and National Guard. Funding related to the training and other specific duties of the AFR is provided by Congress through Reserve Personnel Appropriations (RPA). Funding for the same purposes is provided to the ANG through National Guard Personnel Appropriations (NGPA). Any task completed by a member of the reserve components in support of the active component is funded with MPA, which is the funding source for the active component.[26] As one Major Command official told us, "All we're doing is paying for access to the reserve components."[27]

The annual congressional appropriations state the purposes for which NGPA and RPA may be used. Those purposes include pay, allowances, clothing, subsistence, gratuities, travel, and related expenses for personnel on active duty for training (annual training, additional training, and inactive-duty training). RPA may also be used for other periods of active duty, such as AGR duty, active duty at the seat of government and at headquarters responsible for reserve affairs, to serve on the Air Force Reserve Forces Policy Committee, and to serve as the chief of the AFR. There also are a limited number of operational support missions assigned to the Reserves that may be performed using RPA, such as unit support and funeral honors

---

[24] Interview AF5, senior ANG official, April 11, 2018; Interview AF3, senior U.S. Air Force officers, April 26, 2018.

[25] Interview AF7, ANG official, November 7, 2017.

[26] Dolfini-Reed and Stafford, 2010, p. 12.

[27] Interview AF18, senior Major Command official, May 23, 2018.

support. For ANG personnel, similarly, NGPA provides for training (annual training, additional training, and inactive-duty training), AGR duty, duty at the National Guard Bureau, property and fiscal officer duty, and a limited number of support roles for training operations and training missions assigned to the ANG. Further Operation and Maintenance (O&M) appropriations for the ANG may be used for medical and hospital treatment and related expenses in nonfederal hospitals.[28]

When appropriated funds are used for a purpose other than Congress intended, this noncompliance with the purpose statute can result in violations under the Anti-Deficiency Act.[29] Specifically, the purpose statute prohibits federal agencies from obligations or the expending of federal funds in excess of an appropriation, in addition to accepting voluntary services.[30] A violation of the purpose statute can result in criminal penalties with a fine up to $5,000, imprisonment for up to two years, or both.[31] Generally, this means that RPA and NGPA cannot be used to fund orders for reserve component members for missions assigned to the RegAF, since that is not a stated purpose for those appropriations.

However, under Title 31 U.S.C. Section 1535, commonly referred to as the Economy Act, federal agencies are permitted to procure goods and services from another federal agency in order to obtain economy of scale and eliminate overlapping activities in the federal government. This includes transactions within DoD components.[32] These provisions, therefore, may permit the RegAF to reimburse the ANG or AFR for goods and services rendered, which would then nullify a possible violation under the Anti-Deficiency Act.

---

[28] Public Law 115-31, Consolidated Appropriations Act, 2017, Division C, Department of Defense Appropriations Act, 2017, Title I, Military Personnel.

[29] 31 U.S.C. § 1301.

[30] 31 U.S.C. §§ 1341, 1517.

[31] 31 U.S.C. § 1350.

[32] Department of Defense Regulation 7000.14-R, *Department of Defense Financial Management Regulation*, Volume 11a, Reimbursable Options Policy, Chapter 3, Economy Act Orders, Section 0301, September 2019.

Besides aligning the duty with the purpose of the personnel appropriations, funding plays a role in the planning and utilization of ARC members. A senior ANG official noted in an interview that planning difficulties arise when units have multiyear mission requirements but orders can only be issued from year to year. For example, despite knowing that a unit requires an ARC member for two years, a commander can only issue orders for one year at a time, based on available funding. Thus, service members must wait for the federal budget to pass before knowing whether their positions within the mission requirement will be funded for a second year. Uncertainty over the orders' continuation causes problems with service members' status and forces units to find training days or other alternative mission support paths to maintain ARC members in the unit until funding is officially secured for their position. The uncertainty also contributes to service members' inability to procure, continue, or delay civilian employment should the orders not be issued.[33]

Legal Constraints on Traditional Reservists and Drill Status Guardsmen

There are few restrictions imposed on TRs or DSGs—those reserve component members who, at a minimum, train once a month; complete two weeks of training annually; and may be ordered to active duty in time of war or national emergency. These members may also provide operational support within the limit set for duration of duty under the applicable provision of law. Title 10 also allows reserve component members who are on active duty other than for training to be detailed or assigned to any duty authorized by law for members of the active component, subject to regulations prescribed by the secretary concerned.[34] Since the reserve components are providing support for active missions, that duty is funded with MPA. To do otherwise would result in a purpose violation.

---

[33] Interview AF3, senior U.S. Air Force officers, April 26, 2018.

[34] 10 U.S.C. § 12314.

Legal Constraints on Active-Duty or Full-Time National Guard Duty

Reserve component members on active duty for training or FTNG duty for training may provide operational support if that support is incidental to the training being accomplished. Since the purpose of the duty is training, RPA or, in the case of the National Guard, NGPA is the appropriate funding source—consistent with the purpose of those appropriations.

Congress has recognized that the reserve components are a valuable asset that can be used to provide operational support. As such, it has authorized a limited number of members in each reserve component who may be on active duty or FTNG duty specifically to provide operational support (for other than war or national emergency). The authority under which reserve component members provide this support is either Section 12301(d) of Title 10 for voluntary active duty or Section 502(f)(1)(B) of Title 32 for voluntary FTNG duty. The maximum number of AFR members and ANG members who may be on active duty or FTNG duty at any one time to provide operational support has not changed since January 2006. The ceiling for the AFR has been 14,000, and the ceiling for the ANG has been 16,000.[35] Further, if the Secretary of Defense determines it is in the national interest, he or she may increase the authorized operational support strength ceiling for a reserve component by up to 10 percent of the authorized ceiling for that year.[36] If a service is projected to exceed its authorized active-duty strength, Congress allows the secretary of a military department to increase the active-duty end strength up to 2 percent for that fiscal year.[37] The Secretary of Defense may increase the active-duty strength authorization by not more than 3 percent when the secretary determines that an increase is in the national interest.[38] These increases are not cumulative, however, and if the Secretary of Defense has authorized an increase, any increase by the

---

[35] Public Law 109-163, National Defense Authorization Act for Fiscal Year 2006, Section 415, January 6, 2006, 119 Stat. 3222.

[36] 10 U.S.C. § 115(f)(4).

[37] 10 U.S.C. § 115(g)(1).

[38] 10 U.S.C. § 115(f)(1).

secretary of a military department must be counted as part of the increase authorized by the Secretary of Defense.[39] In other words, the maximum combined end-strength increase shall not exceed 3 percent.

One requirement is associated with the operational support strength ceiling. If a member's order specifies a period of duty greater than three years or if the member's cumulative periods of active duty and FTNG duty exceed 1,095 man-days in the previous 1,460 days, that member must be counted in either the active-duty strength authorization or the AGR end-strength authorization from the day the order specifying a period greater than three years is issued or from the 1,096th day of duty forward.[40] This does not preclude a member from serving or continuing to serve on active duty or FTNG duty to provide operational support; it is simply an end-strength reporting requirement.

Every reserve component has a pool of members who are routinely available to fill mission requirements. Placing a requirement that might constrain this resource, whether that constraint is real or perceived, appears counterproductive to meeting mission requirements. But this approach ignores the demand signal. If a command continuously requires only the employment of reserve component members to perform its mission, that would appear to be an active component requirement that should be addressed through force structure alignment. If a reserve component member (or several members) continues to fill a persistent requirement, then it calls into question whether this should really be an active-duty billet sourced from the active force, not continuously filled by the reserve components unless that mission is assigned to the reserve components. Requiring a command that routinely relies on reserve component personnel to meet mission requirements to submit a waiver in order to continue to fill that requirement would highlight the force structure imbalance. It seems reasonable to use reserve component members as a bridge until force structure is realigned, but not as a permanent solution. This is not to say that the reserve components should no longer fill that requirement when a threshold is reached, but just as in the current procedure, this should require a waiver. During our discussions with senior leaders, several interviewees argued that the current processes

---

[39] 10 U.S.C. § 115(g)(2).

[40] 10 U.S.C. § 115(b)(2).

of asking for MPA and 1,095 man-day waivers were tantamount to hiding RegAF end strength in the ARC.

Legal Constraints on Full-Time Support Personnel

The restrictions on the duties that FTS personnel may perform—both their primary duties and their additional duty—significantly limit the ability of the reserve components to use this personnel resource to provide operational support. While there have been proposals in the past to expand the duties of FTS personnel, those efforts have been met with very limited success. Congress has not been receptive to changes that expand the primary duties of FTS personnel or provide greater flexibility to the additional duties they may perform.

FTS personnel are AGRs and civilian employees who serve as dual-status military technicians, providing full-time, day-to-day support to the reserve component.[41] The law explicitly states the duties that AGRs are authorized to perform. Their primary duties, as prescribed in both Title 10 and Title 32, are OARIT.[42] The law also explicitly states the duties that dual-status military technicians are authorized to perform. The primary duties for Title 10 military technicians are OAIT of the Selected Reserve, or maintaining and repairing supplies and equipment issued to the Selected Reserve or the armed forces.[43] Similarly, the primary duties of Title 32 military technicians are OAIT of the National Guard, or maintaining and repairing supplies issued to the National Guard or the armed forces.[44]

Both AGR personnel and military technicians are authorized to perform certain additional duties, to the extent that those duties do not interfere with their primary duties. Table 4.2 lists the additional duties that AGR personnel and military technicians are authorized to perform.[45]

---

[41] Dual-status military technicians are civilian employees who, as a condition of employment, are required to maintain membership in the Selected Reserve.

[42] 10 U.S.C. §§ 101(d)(6)(A), 12310(a); and 32 U.S.C. § 328.

[43] 10 U.S.C. § 10216(a).

[44] 32 U.S.C. § 709(a).

[45] 10 U.S.C. §§ 12310(b), 10216; and 32 U.S.C. §§ 328, 502, 709.

TABLE 4.2

Additional Duties Air Force Full-Time Support Personnel May Perform

Type of Support	Active Guard and Reserve		Military Technicians	
	Title 10	Title 32	Title 10	Title 32
Operation or mission support	Support operations or missions assigned in whole or part to the reserve components		Support operations or missions assigned in whole or in part to the technician's unit	Support of federal training operations or federal training missions assigned in whole or in part to the technician's unit
President or Secretary of Defense requests		Support operations or missions undertaken by the member's unit at the request of the president or the secretary of defense		Support operations or missions undertaken by the technician's unit at the request of the president or the secretary of defense
Joint unit support	Support operations or missions performed by a unit composed of more than one component of the U.S. Air Force, or a joint force unit that includes one or more reserve component units or a reserve component member whose reserve component assignment is in an element of a joint force unit		Support operations or missions performed by a unit composed of more than one component of the U.S. Air Force, or a joint force unit that includes a member of the technician's component, or a member of the technician's component whose reserve component assignment is in an element of a joint force unit	

Table 4.2—Continued

Type of Support	Active Guard and Reserve		Military Technicians	
	Title 10	Title 32	Title 10	Title 32
Train active, DoD civilians, foreign military	Instruct or train active-duty members, members of foreign military forces, DoD contractor personnel, or DoD civilian employees, but only if such instruction or training is undertaken in the United States, the Commonwealth of Puerto Rico, or possessions of the United States	Support training operations or training missions assigned in whole or in part to the ANG by the secretary of the U.S. Air Force to instruct active-duty military, foreign military, DoD contractor personnel, or DoD civilian employees, but only if such missions or operations are performed in the United States, the Commonwealth of Puerto Rico, or possessions of the United States	Instruct or train active-duty members, members of foreign military forces, DoD contractor personnel, or DoD civilian employees, but only if such instruction or training is undertaken in the United States, the Commonwealth of Puerto Rico, or possessions of the United States	Instruct or train active-duty members, members of foreign military forces, DoD contractor personnel, or DoD civilian employees, but only if such instruction or training is undertaken in the United States, the Commonwealth of Puerto Rico, or possessions of the United States
Headquarters assignments	Advise the secretary of defense, secretary of the U.S. Air Force, Joint Chiefs of Staff, and combatant commanders on reserve component matters			

SOURCES: 10 U.S.C. § 12310; 32 U.S.C. § 328; 32 U.S.C. § 501(F)(2); 10 U.S.C. § 10216; and 32 U.S.C. § 709.

During our interviews, we repeatedly heard confusion about what the primary responsibilities are for FTS personnel (in particular, AGRs), as well as confusion about the so-called 51-percent rule that requires FTS personnel to spend the majority of their time conducting their primary responsibilities (OARIT for AGRs and OAIT for military technicians). This rule was clearly perceived as a barrier to utilization of FTS personnel for sustained active-duty operational support missions. However, we also heard that AGRs have played a key role in the development of emerging mission sets, such as space operations, and that it would have been hard to grow the mission set so quickly without utilizing AGRs. Yet one commander also acknowledged that there are a lot of myths about how AGRs can and cannot be utilized.[46] A senior U.S. Air Force leader also told us that FTS personnel are essentially the piece of the reserve component that is an operational force.[47]

Previous Changes Recommended to Eliminate Barriers to Providing Operational Support

Recent reviews by the Office of the Air Force Judge Advocate General, the NCSAF, and the RFPB examined the legal and policy avenues through which reserve component forces could support active-duty missions and suggested changes that would provide for easier access to the reserve components and greater flexibility to employ reserve component forces.

The NCSAF specifically recommended that in order to gain maximum benefit from reserve component forces, the U.S. Air Force should include in all future budget submissions to Congress a specific funding line for "'operational support by the ARC' to clearly identify and program those funds intended to permit routine, periodic employment of the active component either as volunteers or under the authority of 10 U.S.C. §12304b."[48] Further, the NCSAF recommended that members ordered to active duty under

---

[46] Interview AF11, U.S. Department of the Air Force space operations commander, February 28, 2018.

[47] Interview AF13, senior AFR official, June 9, 2018.

[48] NCSAF, 2014, p. 8.

Section 12304b should not be counted in calculating authorized strength in members on active duty under Title 10 or any other statutes.[49] The RFPB made the same suggestion in its 2016 report.[50] RAND, however, has found that routine, recurring use of involuntary activation measures to meet operational demands remains untested, and its effects are unknown.[51] The concern is overstressing the reserve component force by imposing an operations tempo that could become detrimental to both recruiting and retention. As one senior U.S. Air Force leader told us, "The RegAF keeps asking us for more, and there will be a tipping point. What worries me most is that we are breaking the Reserve due to the stress on families and employers."[52]

In response to a request for a legal opinion to allow ARC members to provide personnel support to RegAF members, as well as ARC members as part of an active-reserve integrated force support squadron (FSS),[53] the Office of the Air Force Judge Advocate cited four instances under current law in which ARC members can specifically provide such services to RegAF members:

1. Certain drill-status and full-time ANG and FTS members in duty status under Title 32 of the U.S.C.—
    a. may perform FSS services for training, even if doing so incidentally benefits active component, or
    b. may perform FSS services to RegAF members under the "de minimis" doctrine.
2. If the FSS mission is formally assigned to the ARC, FTS ARC members (only includes AFR AGR personnel) in duty status under Title 10 may provide the full spectrum of FSS services to RegAF members, as long as those services do not interfere with the ARC members' main duties.

---

[49] 10 U.S.C. § 12304(d).

[50] RFPB, 2016, pp. 54–55.

[51] Robbert et al., 2014.

[52] Interview AF12, senior AFR official, June 19, 2018.

[53] FSSs provide military and civilian personnel, manpower and organization, education, professional military education, career enhancement, airman and family support services, and quality-of-life programs for military and civilian members and families.

3. ARC members in total force integration units may provide proportionate support to RegAF members.

4. ARC members in active-duty operational support status under Title 10 U.S.C. § 12314 may provide the full spectrum of FSS services to RegAF members. However, the Office of the Air Force Judge Advocate General cautioned against interpreting the statute to broadly refer to the Reserves, because it cannot be used to relieve a Title 10 AGR from the mandated requirement to perform OARIT for the reserve component.[54]

The Office of the Air Force Judge Advocate suggested in 2013 that obtaining legislative relief from the restrictions for FTS personnel would likely be difficult.[55]

The memorandum from the Office of the Air Force Judge Advocate also offered several approaches to reducing or lifting statutory restrictions on the use of FTS personnel and described the obstacles to those approaches succeeding. Generally speaking, those approaches included expanding the duties that AGRs and military technicians are allowed to perform.

- Include the specific operational support mission in the additional duties that FTS personnel may perform. This approach would provide a little more flexibility, but those additional duties would still be subject to the "not to interfere" clause.
- Remove the "not to interfere" clause for the additional duties that FTS personnel may perform. However, this could certainly call into question the entire purpose of FTS personnel by possibly diminishing the support they would provide to reserve component units.
- Allow FTS personnel to perform activities for the total force, not just the reserve component, as part of their primary duties of organizing, administering, recruiting (AGRs only), instructing, and training. This could be accomplished by either removing the phrase "the Reserve

---

[54] Office of the Air Force Judge Advocate, "Legal Review—Allowing Reserve Component (RC) Members to Provide Force Support Squadron (FSS) Services to Active Component (AC) Members," July 19, 2013, p. 1.

[55] Office of the Air Force Judge Advocate, 2013, pp. 10–13.

Components/the Selected Reserve/the National Guard," as applicable, in the description of their primary duties or adding the phrase "or the armed forces," similar to the description of the duties of military technicians, who are permitted to maintain and repair supplies or equipment.[56]

Fundamentally, each approach is intended to provide the secretary concerned with greater flexibility to manage and employ the forces under his or her jurisdiction. This concept is similar to the 2008 consolidation of special pay, incentive pay, and bonus authorities of the uniformed services[57] and the 2011 consolidation and reform of travel and transportation authorities of the uniformed services.[58] A more recent reform called for by Congress is the consolidation of authorities to order members of the reserve components of the armed forces to perform duty.[59]

While Congress has supported other reform initiatives, it has been less supportive of legislative proposals to expand the duties that FTS personnel may perform. In 2015, the U.S. Air Force proposed legislation that would allow a limited number of AFR and ANG AGRs and military technicians to instruct or train members of the armed forces on active duty or members of foreign military forces. This proposal was submitted by DoD and enacted in the National Defense Authorization Act for Fiscal Year 2016 as a temporary authority. Some relief might be achieved if duty status reform is enacted as described in Chapter Five.

---

[56] 10 U.S.C. § 10216(a)(1)(C) states that Title 10 military technicians may maintain and repair "supplies or equipment issued to Selected Reserve or the armed forces," while 32 U.S.C. § 709(a)(2) states that Title 32 military technicians may maintain and repair "supplies issued to the National Guard or the armed forces," yet the Office of the Air Force Judge Advocate has asserted that Title 32 military technicians may also perform maintenance and repair on equipment, citing the definition of "supplies" found in 10 U.S.C. 101(a)(14). Office of the Air Force Judge Advocate, 2013, p. 9.

[57] Public Law 110-181, National Defense Authorization Act for Fiscal Year 2008, Section 661, January 28, 2008.

[58] Public Law 112-81, National Defense Authorization Act for Fiscal Year 2012, Section 631, December 31, 2011.

[59] Public Law 115-91, National Defense Authorization Act for Fiscal Year 2018, Section 513, December 12, 2017.

Conclusion

We found few statutory limitations for employing TR and DSG members to support operational missions, whether for war or national emergency, or to provide operational support for requirements other than those of war or national emergency. The only requirement for National Guard and Reserve members providing operational support is the end-strength reporting for a member who exceeds 1,095 man-days in the previous 1,460 days, or whose orders specify a period greater than three years. This strength accounting requirement does not apply to reserve component members ordered to active duty without their consent to support preplanned CCMD missions. Duty status reform, discussed later in this report, if enacted, could provide greater flexibility for employing ARC members to support RegAF and CCMD missions and requirements.

As concluded in a 2014 RAND study[60] and validated during our research, legislative relief is necessary in order to provide greater flexibility in utilizing AGRs and military technicians as a ready asset to support operational missions, whether for the active or reserve component. While there are several options that could be considered to expand the duties AGRs and military technicians could perform, a significant shift in their underlying purpose would have to take place to gain the support of Congress.

The next chapter provides an analysis of resource and personnel policies that constrain the utilization of ARC members for sustained active-duty missions.

---

[60] See Robbert et al., 2014.

CHAPTER FIVE

Resource, Policy, and Permeability Constraints to Utilization of Air Reserve Component Members

In addition to the legal constraints described in the previous chapter, certain personnel and resource policies and the processes derived from them also constrain utilization of ARC members. These constraints emanate from guidance, directives, instructions, memoranda, and other policy documents at multiple levels: DoD, U.S. Air Force, AFR, ANG, and unit. While in the course of our policy review, we found that there are few instances where policy is written in a way that deliberately aims to limit ARC support to the RegAF, we discovered that the lack of clarity in guidance, conflicting direction, and misinterpretation among stakeholders all pose substantial policy barriers to ARC support of active-duty missions and permeability between the two components. Further, lack of cross-component understanding of the RegAF and the ARC contributes to the entrenchment of cultural barriers that also serve to hinder effective ARC utilization.

Underlining these challenges, policies tend to conceive of the ARC as a strategic rather than operational reserve and do not account for how reliant on the ARC the U.S. Air Force has become. As one National Guard official told us, "The Air Force can't continue looking at MPA issues as a temporary solution to a temporary problem."[1] Several interviewees observed that the U.S. Air Force approaches the ARC as a way to "patch holes" rather than

---

[1] Interview AF7, ANG official, November 7, 2017.

address manpower issues more holistically.[2] Others stressed that while volunteerism currently enables the RegAF to fill its necessary billets, it is variable and sensitive to economic trends, and may not continue to be sufficient into the future.

The following are the major resource, policy, and permeability constraints to ARC utilization:

- resource constraints
  - lack of adequate and predictable funding
  - volatility added to budget-planning process by continuing resolutions (CRs)
  - funding disconnected from end strength
  - rigidity of resource management processes
  - inflexibility of budgeting process
- policy constraints
  - ambiguous FTS personnel policies
  - confusion over 1,095 man-day rule
  - lack of clarity and flexibility on joint travel regulations
  - burdensome waiver processes
- permeability constraints
  - separate pay and benefits systems
  - challenges with reserve unit reaffiliation and career progression
  - cumbersome scrolling process
  - lack of cross-component understanding.

Next, we examine each of these constraints, as well as the experiences of the other services in managing this subpopulation of their reserve components that conduct active-duty missions.

Resource Constraints

A recurring theme in our review of the literature and in interviews was the impact of resource constraints on the RegAF's ability to leverage the ARC effectively. Two major themes emerged in our analysis of resource chal-

---

[2] Interview AF5, senior ANG official, April 11, 2018.

lenges: lack of adequate and predictable funding, and the rigidity of resource management processes.

Lack of Adequate and Predictable Funding

Insufficient funding appears to be one of the leading challenges to the ARC's ability to provide support to the RegAF. The 2014 NCSAF report stresses this point:

> The Commission repeatedly has heard formal and informal testimony, supported by written reports from ARC leaders, that the ARC can do more if sufficient funding is provided. The Commission also has received testimony that "man-day" or "man-year" funding, originally in the base budget to fund ARC support for active duty missions, sometimes has become unavailable to operational commands because it is transferred to meet other priorities.[3]

The NCSAF further highlights the specific need to fully fund orders to active duty for preplanned missions in support of the CCMDs: "In order to gain maximum benefit from the reserve components, the Air Force must program sufficient operational support funding to permit utilization of individuals and units through volunteerism or under the authority of 10 U.S.C. § 12304b."[4] One senior ANG official noted that the chief challenges are "money and MPA resourcing to start. If we don't have money to pay people and bring them in on orders, that is barrier number one."[5]

Further, while current guidance (Air Force Instruction [AFI] 36-2619) directs O&M funds to support travel and per diem costs associated with MPA requirements, the execution of these funds might not necessarily synchronize as planned and budgeted. Even if MPA funds exist and are sufficient to support a requirement, Major Commands may prioritize their O&M funding in a manner that no longer coincides with the planned MPA days. This potentially limits the pool of available members for the MPA

---

[3] NCSAF, 2014, p. 21.

[4] NCSAF, 2014, pp. 18–19.

[5] Interview AF8, U.S. Air Force official familiar with total force policies, November 9, 2017.

requirement to local volunteers, contributing to the issue of access.[6] One interviewee suggested that O&M be tied to MPA.[7]

Limited funding also forces some commands to rely on local ARC members as often as possible, even if individuals located farther away might be better suited for the position. If an ARC member resides less than 50 miles from his or her duty station, the unit saves resources by not having to pay per diem or lodging for that service member. This issue speaks more broadly to the challenge that, to provide for RegAF requirements, the ARC has two options: MPA combined with volunteerism, or involuntary mobilization. For ARC members who left the RegAF because of the strain of frequent mobilizations, the second option is less than ideal and could lead to difficulty recruiting prior active-duty service members into the ARC. Also, while several interviewees noted that volunteerism is currently sufficient, there is a common fear that rates of volunteerism will soon drop. One AFR officer we interviewed expanded on this point:

> There is also the issue that beyond MPA for funding, I have to rely on people to volunteer. The other way is to mobilize. You cannot mobilize unless there is an authorization, which requires a named operation. In order to create workarounds, we'll sometimes use RPA with the hope that it will be backfilled by MPA. For the case of full-scale war, my force is ready. But the day-to-day demands are where it is hard, and we are underresourced.[8]

Volatility Added to the Budget-Planning Process by Continuing Resolutions

Finally, a resourcing issue that significantly affects the utilization of ARC members is funding unpredictability, specifically Congress's use of CRs to fund the federal government. Many of our interviewees noted that the reliance on CRs adds more volatility to the planning process—especially when

---

[6] Interview AF2, U.S. Department of the Air Force space operations commander, January 9, 2018.

[7] Interview AF11, U.S. Department of the Air Force space operations commander, February 28, 2018.

[8] Interview AF1, senior AFR official, June 19, 2018.

MPA allocations are delayed. The lack of predictability that CRs introduce to the orders process leaves some feeling responsible for a process that they cannot control. According to one U.S. Air Force personnel official, "Congress owns and controls that space, so we are left with assuming risk."[9] Part of this risk directly affects orders going into the next fiscal year. As one senior U.S. Air Force officer told us, "If we don't have a full budget, we have to let people go at the end of the year."[10]

One particularly problematic impact of CRs is that they can challenge ARC members' relationships with their civilian employers. By law, employees must notify their civilian employer when the employee will be absent for work to perform military duty.[11] As one official told us,

> Continuing resolutions are killing us. We need a budget that's dependable. For instance, CRs are extremely problematic for TRs. If there is a CR at the beginning of the fiscal year, TRs usually go back to their employers and then by the time the CR breaks, the TRs are tied up long term with their employers. Also, by the time we get a dump of funding in the summer, there are not enough days left in the fiscal year to spend all those days.[12]

Some of our ANG respondents reported that CRs cause additional funding problems because the O&M budget is relatively small in the first place, and depot and maintenance costs, combined with a reimbursement process where National Guard aviation units supporting active-duty missions pay for flying costs up front and get reimbursed later, consume all available funding from CRs.[13] With full budgets and more predictability instead of piecemeal CRs, National Guard units could spread those costs across the full fiscal year.

---

[9] Interview AF9, U.S. Air Force personnel official, November 8, 2017.

[10] Interview AF5, U.S. Air Force senior official, April 11, 2018.

[11] Interview AF8, U.S. Air Force official familiar with total force policy, November 9, 2017.

[12] Interview AF2, U.S. Department of the Air Force space operations commander, January 9, 2018.

[13] Interview AF4, senior ANG official, April 11, 2018.

Funding Disconnected from End Strength

While Congress annually authorizes the strength ceiling for operational support, funding for providing operational support is not automatically included in the budget and is not tied to end strength. However, since the release of the report from NCSAF, the U.S. Air Force has included in its annual military personnel budget request full funding for active duty for operational support provided by the ARC. There remains, however, a mismatch between the personnel resource in the ARC and the funding resource in the RegAF.

Rigidity of Resource Management Processes

Beyond limited and unpredictable resources, we identified inefficiencies in existing resource management processes that exacerbate the ARC's challenges in providing sustained support to the RegAF. Funding for the National Guard and Reserve remains rooted in the strategic reserve construct; it does not necessarily support an operational reserve. NGPA and RPA are for training and support requirements specific to the reserve components. Those funds cannot be used to provide operational support to the active component. This puts the reserve components in the position of providing the manpower with no way to pay for that manpower. The result is that while the National Guard and Reserve are tasked to support an active mission and are ready to deploy, they cannot execute the mission until the funding is provided from the active component.[14] There remains a mismatch between the personnel resource in the ARC and the funding resource in the RegAF.

---

[14] This is unlike filling the requirement from the active component. When an active component member fills a requirement, funding comes from MPA—regardless of whether the member is supporting an active component or reserve component requirement. The member simply remains on active duty as part of the authorized active-duty strength. But if a reserve component member fills a requirement, the funding source is determined by which component generated the requirement. If it is an active component requirement, then funding is from MPA, unless any support provided is simply incidental to training being conducted. If it is a reserve component requirement, then the funding is from RPA or NGPA. In other words, funding is based on which component benefits from the support being provided, not the component providing the personnel to meet that requirement.

Several interviewees noted frustration with current processes and reported the need to cobble together types of funding and authorities in order to execute their mission. One interviewee suggested that a solution to this patchwork would be to eliminate their distinctions entirely, stating, "On the resources side, I think we should just give the A3 [U.S. Air Force operations directorate] a slush fund and let them appropriate and manage the MPA budget."[15] While such a proposal might not be feasible, the frustration with having to navigate the multiple authorities and processes associated with each was clear among many interviewees. One official said, "We end up playing games with the money."[16] This cobbling together of funds and authorities not only is challenging for units but also can create complicated situations where active component and reserve component funds are "mixed" and RPA- or NGPA-funded personnel are performing active-duty work or are on active-duty orders.[17]

Inflexible Nature of the Budgeting Process

Another key resource management problem is the relatively inflexible nature of the budgeting process. Operational requirements often mean that units need to make changes in the year of execution, which might differ from what was in the POM, the DoD programming document that communicates the services' final resource allocation decisions. This inability to predict future budgeting needs also stymies the U.S. Department of the Air Force's ability to prioritize emerging requirements and can be particularly problematic when considering resource tradeoffs.[18] The NCSAF also called out the challenges posed by this rigidity in budgeting, stating, "Congress should allow DoD increased flexibility in applying budget cuts across budget categories, including installations."[19]

Certain programs, such as the Voluntary Limited Period of Active Duty (VLPAD) program, are particularly sensitive to this budgeting inflexibility.

---

[15] Interview AF8, U.S. Air Force official familiar with total force policies, November 9, 2017.

[16] Interview AF5, senior U.S. Air Force official, April 11, 2018.

[17] Interview AF4, senior U.S. Air Force official, April 11, 2018.

[18] Interview AF9, U.S. Air Force personnel official, November 8, 2017.

[19] NCSAF, 2014, p. 26.

The VLPAD allows units to bring ARC members into unfilled billets for specific active-duty specialties that are facing personnel shortages. The U.S. Air Force tightly controls the number of VLPAD positions to 250 and restricts the AFSCs that qualify to access VLPAD to those contending with critical personnel vacancies based on current requirements. However, the U.S. Air Force is expected to prioritize its personnel requirements through its manpower system, which fluctuates with the budgeting cycle, which in turn provides the requirements that the assignment process tries to fill. As a result, the U.S. Air Force often cannot accurately predict those requirements because of fluctuations in operational need. This results in utilization of programs like VLPAD, which are intended to be used as a stop-gap measure rather than a permanent solution.[20]

Additionally, competition for both baseline budget and OCO funding incentivizes units to continually increase their budget requests regardless of actual need. This not only muddies the budgeting and planning process but could obfuscate true requirements. A U.S. Air Force personnel official told us,

> There is a culture of you never turn anything back in and always request more, whether that be the Air Force baseline budget or OCO funds. Every year, it's a game of "extortionary chicken." But it's the commands and [CCMDs] that have the best sense of priorities for who receives OCO funds. I think it's all really an Air Force management resources problem.[21]

Mismatches in timelines between the duration of orders and the obligation of funds also cause stress for both individuals and units attempting to fill long-term orders. An example of this difficulty is in the process of how orders become funded in the U.S. Air Force's order-writing system for ANG members. One interviewee reported,

> When longer orders are input in to AROWS [Air National Guard Reserve Order Writing System], they obligate funds immediately and consume the budget for the entire order. This is an issue because the

---

[20] Interview AF6, AFR official, February 1, 2018.

[21] Interview AF9, U.S. Air Force personnel official, November 8, 2017.

current budgeting system calls for a quarterly authority of funds, while many orders are written for longer periods. Therefore, the orders are obligating funds that have not necessarily been authorized yet. This particularly affects part-timers who need some commitment of employment from the Air Force. . . . The workaround is that folks cut back on the length of orders and spread them out, but this impacts the member's benefits and fudges reporting.[22]

Finally, the distribution of funds on a quarterly basis also affects the ability to employ ARC members. Depending on when funds are authorized, the ARC might not have funds to cut orders or, alternatively, if they are authorized late in the fiscal year, might be challenged to obligate the funds before they expire. Further, the availability of funding might not coincide with the availability of personnel (or the right personnel) and can create uncertainty for ARC members who need to plan ahead for family, work, or other personal reasons.[23]

Policy Constraints

U.S. Air Force policies, derived in many cases from statute and DoD policies, can limit utilization of the ARC for active-duty missions in two main ways: ambiguous language that leads to diverse interpretations of policy, and prohibitive requirements at the unit and individual levels.

U.S. Air Force policies are most limiting in their tendency to be ambiguous and lead to uneven interpretation across units and components. Through our research, we identified three main policies with issues regarding clarity: the use of AGRs, the 1,095 man-day reporting requirement, and Joint Travel Regulations (JTR). Misunderstandings over the application of these policies in some cases have already limited access to the ARC for active-duty missions. As the use of AGRs, the 1,095 man-day reporting requirement, and the JTR represent significant policy areas of concern for

---

[22] Interview AF2, U.S. Department of the Air Force space operations commander, January 9, 2018.

[23] Interview AF2, U.S. Department of the Air Force space operations commander, January 9, 2018.

the ARC, the following sections provide a brief overview of each, including relevant law and policy direction, process implementation, and additional requirements, such as how waiver processes affect ARC utilization.

Ambiguous Full-Time Support Personnel Policies

Ambiguity in U.S. Air Force policy outlining the responsibilities of FTS personnel leads to confusion over the amount of time FTS personnel (in particular AGRs) are required to spend conducting their primary duties. First, law and policy direct the use of AGR members through the delineation of their primary responsibilities. As described in Chapter Three, the primary responsibilities for AGRs are "organizing, administering, recruiting, instructing, or training (OARIT) [of] the reserve components." AFI 36-2132, *Volume 2, Active Guard/Reserve (AGR) Program*, describes the implementation of the AGR program, which allows military individuals to volunteer for active duty to carry out these defined responsibilities. The related DoD Instruction, 1205.18, *Full-Time Support (FTS) to the Reserve Components*, outlines the limitations for AGR duties. According to the policy, AGRs are permitted to perform duties outside of their primary responsibilities, but they must not interfere with those responsibilities. The policy also highlights the limitation of using AGRs for deployments: "Regardless of the role of an AGR, the law severely limits AGR deployments that are not in direct support of reserve missions. The congressional intent in this law is clear and specifically drives the following AGR deployment policy."[24]

The policies regarding the use of AGRs appeared to cause some confusion over how much time AGRs can dedicate to duties other than OARIT. Policies focus on the primary duties of an AGR, which may lead some personnel managers to believe that AGRs are not permitted to perform any other duties that they might be assigned. But this is not the case. The law also prescribes, and limits, the additional duties that AGRs are permitted to perform, as shown in Table 4.2.

---

[24] Air Force Instruction 36-2132, *Volume 2, Active Guard/Reserve (AGR) Program*, February 10, 2014, pp. 4, 5–6, 15; Department of Defense Instruction 1205.18, *Full-Time Support (FTS) to the Reserve Components*, June 5, 2020; 10 U.S.C. § 101; 10 U.S.C. § 12310; and 32 U.S.C. § 328.

Some of our interviewees stated that the policy requires that AGRs spend at least 51 percent of their time performing their primary duties. The 51-percent allotment is derived from the idea that AGRs' "primary" OARIT responsibilities must make up a majority of their time. The OARIT requirements can and have been used as a limitation as to what an AGR can perform while on active duty or FTNG duty, which hinders the full utilization of some ARC members. As a U.S. Department of the Air Force space operations official noted during an interview, "When AGRs are needed to perform the mission, they need to justify the type of work to utilize them for more than half-time to support active component activities. There should be more flexibility to using the AGRs as needed."[25] However, the policy itself does not specify the amount of time an AGR can spend conducting duties other than OARIT, nor does it prohibit an AGR from performing duties outside of their OARIT responsibilities. In fact, as noted earlier, policy specifically states that AGRs can perform duties other than their OARIT responsibilities, as long as they do not interfere with them. Some within the U.S. Department of the Air Force are aware of this, as one senior U.S. Air Force official stated during an interview, "AGRs are to take care of their OARIT roles first, but not at a specific percentage."[26]

Confusion over 1,095 Man-Day Rule

Confusion over the 1,095 man-day reporting requirement in U.S. Air Force policy centers on the misconception that the requirement prohibits members from serving more than 1,095 man-days out of the previous 1,460 man-day period, when the policy only requires the tracking of those who may exceed 1,095 man-days of active service. To better understand how this misconception formed, this section describes the policy and the perceptions surrounding it.

Law and policy require the military services to track and report the number of active-duty members counted toward the total end strength authorized per service each year. U.S.C. Title 10, Section 115, requires the tracking of reserve component members who serve in active duty longer

---

[25] Interview AF2, U.S. Department of the Air Force space operations commander, January 9, 2018, p. 5.

[26] Interview AF11, senior U.S. Air Force officer, February 28, 2018.

than 1,095 man-days of the previous 1,460 man-days and their inclusion in end-strength reporting. Accordingly, the U.S. Department of the Air Force must be aware of how many individuals may attain this amount of service in a given year to ensure accurate end-strength accounting. To carry out the law's requirements, both DoD and the U.S. Air Force issued policies to guide implementation. DoD Instruction 1215.06, *Uniform Reserve, Training, and Retirement Categories for the Reserve Components*, details the requirement and highlights the important fact that the potential for someone to exceed the 1,095 man-day mark does not mean that the individual must deny or be prevented from taking orders. The policy states that the purpose of the 1,095 man-day requirement is to ensure correct reporting to inform the optimal end-strength accounting between active and reserve components: "Neither law nor DoD policy requires any reserve component service member to leave voluntary Active Duty under section 12301(d) (OS duty) of Reference (d) [Title 10, U.S.C.] after 1,095 man-days. However, consideration will be given to documenting long-term tours as full-time requirement billets (active component, AGR, or civilian)."[27]

U.S. Air Force policy on the 1,095 man-day reporting outlines the service's processes for meeting the requirement. The types of tours that must be counted toward the reporting requirement include active duty under Title 10 U.S.C. § 12301(d), or FTNG duty under Title 32 U.S.C. § 502(f)(2) (or any combination thereof). Funding sources do not change the reporting requirements, as both RPA- or NGPA-funded positions and MPA-funded positions count toward the 1,095 man-day requirement. U.S. Air Force policy also outlines the process by which the U.S. Air Force permits continued service by reserve component members beyond the 1,095 man-day mark. If a member is found to be within the 1,095 man-day threshold, meaning the member's current tour will require him or her to pass the 1,095 man-day allotment within the previous 1,460 man-day period, then a waiver must be approved by SAF/MR before the member can receive orders. Those requesting waivers must provide significant justification as to why the specific reserve member must remain in his or her position after the 1,095 man-days.[28] (See Table 5.1 for how waivers are scored.)

---

[27] 10 U.S.C. § 115; DoDI 1215.06, 2014, pp. 42–43.

[28] AFI 36-2619, 2014, pp. 31–36; Air Force Instruction 2254, *Volume 1, Reserve Personnel Participation*, May 26, 2010, pp. 51–52.

TABLE 5.1

U.S. Air Force 1,095 Man-Day Day Waiver Review Scoring

Weighted Criteria	Point Value			
	1	2	3	4
U.S. Air Force mission priorities	2	3	4	5
Same AFSC, same local area	<735	735-1,000	1,001–1,095	>1,095
Previous waivers	No		Yes	
Stressed career field list	Yes		No	
Total ADOS days	1,096–1,187	1,188–1,279	1,280–1,371	1,372–1,460

SOURCE: AFI 36-2619, p. 34, Table 5.1.

The instruction further provides key dates for the 1,095 ADOS accounting process. On a monthly basis, supported commands and staffs or agency panels convene to evaluate waiver requests. If an individual was previously denied a request but would like to appeal to Headquarters Air Force, those requests must be filed by the 5th of the month, with decisions forwarded back to commands by the 15th of the month (with the assumption that packages are submitted at least 60 days before tour start). By June 1, all members who will cross the 1,095 man-day threshold after September 29 must submit their requests. By July 1, supported commands must review total ADOS time for members nearing the 1,095 or 1,460 man-day threshold during the following fiscal year. By July 16, all members denied their waiver requests must be alerted that they must be off tour no later than September 29 of that year.[29]

For the National Guard, the states producing Army National Guard or ANG orders are the authorities responsible for monitoring potential violations of the 1,095 man-day rule. Individuals requesting a waiver submit their packets through the National Guard Manpower and Personnel Directorate (NG-J1), who completes a cost analysis and recommends approval or disapproval.[30]

---

[29] AFI 36-2619, 2014, p. 35.

[30] Chief National Guard Bureau Manual 1302.01, *Orders Guidance for Counter Drug Aviation Personnel Migrating to Support Enhanced Southwest Border Security Operations*, July 26, 2013, p. A-3.

In our discussions with relevant U.S. Air Force personnel, varying perspectives arose over the 1,095 man-day reporting requirement. Some interviewees viewed the need to report and request a waiver for the 1,095 man-days as an actual limit to using ARC members beyond the 1,095 man-day period. As one senior U.S. Air Force official affirmed, "When people hit 1,095, they are done. Off-limits, you cannot touch them again. . . . We also have people that would hit 1,095 while they were deployed and you had to send them home."[31] Another confirmed that they understood the 1,095 man-day reporting requirement but saw how other members viewed it as a limit, rather than just a reporting requirement.[32] On the other hand, others viewed the requirement as necessary and without issue. They argued that once waivers reached the Pentagon, they would likely be approved and should not hinder accessibility of ARC members. As one interviewee with knowledge of the approval process stated, "At lower levels, people forget that if a 1,095 man-day waiver finds its way into the building, it will get approved."[33] An ANG official similarly noted,

> But 1,095 waivers are approved by SAF/MR as an individual name and package. Their standing policy is that they won't disapprove 1,095 waivers. They need to know the numbers concerning 1,095 waivers for end-strength accountability, as they are required in Title 10, Section 115, to track the number of personnel and document the reasons why they went over 1,095 days.[34]

Such reflections indicate that, while the official policy as stipulated in AFI 36-2619 requires that members scoring 14 or more should be "disapproved unless justification based on mission requirements is appropriately documented," in practice, SAF/MR is willing to provide such justification and documentation.

---

[31] Interview AF10, senior U.S. Air Force official, May 31, 2018.

[32] Interview AF11, senior U.S. Air Force officer, February 28, 2018.

[33] Interview AF8, U.S. Air Force official familiar with total force policies, November 9, 2017, p. 2.

[34] Interview AF7, ANG official, November 7, 2017.

Lack of Clarity and Flexibility on Joint Travel Regulations

Another policy that creates misunderstandings at the unit and individual levels is the DoD JTR manual, which provides guidance and instruction on travel, housing, transportation, and cost-of-living allowances for DoD employees. While the document is quite comprehensive and over 700 pages in length, inconsistent application of the regulations within it appears to cause confusion for the U.S. Air Force, inhibiting effective access of the ARC. The JTR is not necessarily updated when the services update their own policy guidance, which adds to the potential for confusion.

DoD appears to recognize these challenges and has made recent attempts to simplify the JTR and the application of travel regulations across the services. In 2017, the Defense Travel Management Office began a multiphase process to simplify the JTR, including a full rewrite of the document to make it simpler and easier to comprehend.[35] In its justification for the update, the office affirmed that "travel policies are complex, customer issues prevail, and processes are inefficient."[36] It also presented a list of modernization and sustainment initiatives for the Defense Travel System in 2017, which several interviewees noted is a cumbersome system that requires substantial time to process orders and travel vouchers.[37] In addition to the policy ambiguities identified previously, specific requirements included within the JTR inhibit the effective use of the ARC.

Temporary Duty Versus Permanent Change-of-Station Orders

JTR policy challenges often revolve around the distinctions between temporary duty (TDY) and permanent change-of-station (PCS) orders. The U.S. Air Force policy stems from federal policy found within the JTR, Chapter Three, Section 0303. The TDY limitation policy states that reserve component members traveling outside their duty location for less than 180 days

---

[35] Defense Travel Management Office, "The New Joint Travel Regulations," 2017 Gov-Travels Symposium, March 1, 2017b.

[36] Defense Travel Management Office, "Defense Travel System Modernization and Sustainment Initiatives," slide deck, 2017a; Defense Travel Management Office, 2017b.

[37] Interview AF3, senior U.S. Air Force officers, April 26, 2018. See also Interview AF1, senior AFR official, June 19, 2018.

must receive TDY orders, and thus receive travel and local per diem allowances for each of those days. If members' orders are for longer than 180 days, however, their status switches to PCS, which provides for relocation benefits but does not authorize local per diem allowances. This may be difficult for some ARC members, as they often do not want to, or cannot, move from their current community because of family or employment commitments. As a result, in order to accept active-duty orders, reserve component members taking long-term active-duty orders outside their area are often faced with choosing either to bear the financial burden of maintaining two homes or to uproot their families for the duration of their orders.

This issue is particularly restraining for ARC members because a primary benefit of reserve affiliation is greater career choice and flexibility, specifically in location of assignments so that reserve component members may choose where they live and how far they must travel to perform military duty. One senior U.S. Air Force official noted this as a reason why individual service members sometimes decide not to continue their reserve component service: "I think orders and pay issues are big disincentives, along with leadership challenges. . . . A lot of people go to the Reserve or Guard because they want to determine where they live."[38] National Guard members may particularly wish to remain within their local communities.[39] One respondent described how this factor affects the ANG in particular, but the same reasoning can also be applied to AFR members:

> If you're used to working and staying in one place like most Guard members, you're not going to move somewhere for just six months. You only move if can do so temporarily. . . . Many guardsmen get off of active duty because they were tired of moving around [so] being told they have to PCS becomes an issue. They are dealing with civilian employers too, which makes things difficult. Especially if you work for a small company, being gone 6 to 12 months causes issues, and they can't make up pay and promotion differentials.[40]

---

[38] Interview AF8, senior U.S. Air Force official familiar with total force policies, November 9, 2017.

[39] Interview AF4, senior ANG official, April 11, 2018.

[40] Interview AF4, senior ANG official, April 11, 2018.

These trade-offs are particularly challenging to ARC members who maintain civilian employment when not activated. Whether volunteering or facing involuntary mobilization orders, reserve component members employed in the civilian sector must balance their service with their employer's needs and also manage the financial ramifications of going on orders. In some cases, the reserve component member's civilian salary exceeds his or her military pay and allowances, which presents a challenge and possibly a disincentive for some members. Some employers, including the federal government and some state governments, support eligible employees who are activated on orders by paying the difference between their military and civilian salaries or even full civilian salaries. For federal civilian employees ordered to active duty in support of a contingency operation, their employing agency is required by law to pay the difference between their civilian salary and their military pay and allowances.[41] While the policy is very limited in its effectiveness for long-term orders, federal employees are also eligible to collect their full civilian salary in addition to their military compensation for up to 15 days each year. But beyond these two provisions, there is no other legal requirement to make up the difference in pay.[42]

A program called the Reserve Income Replacement Program[43] offers this differential pay under specific conditions that only apply to certain long-term involuntary mobilizations and excludes a large number of reserve component members taking active-duty orders because they never meet the eligibility requirement for the differential pay. One interviewee stated that the applications for this pay are submitted through the service member's unit, so "it's up to the unit commander to offer civilian pay differential."[44] The law requires that a member who meets the eligibility requirements receive the additional pay. Further, there is no law to require civilian employers to make up any pay gap. Because of the narrow scope of the federal differential pay programs, the civilian salary–military duty pay gap and the possibility of incurring out-of-pocket expenses because of the PCS requirement may

---

[41] 5 U.S.C. § 5538.

[42] 5 U.S.C. § 6323.

[43] 37 U.S.C. § 910.

[44] Interview AF7, ANG official, November 7, 2017.

discourage members from taking orders, and narrow the available reserve population to those whose personal financial circumstances allow them to take orders, potentially missing the best reserve component member for the position.[45]

Temporary Duty–Specific Challenges

The JTR also introduces constraints and challenges specific to TDY orders. First, the cost of TDY allowances can create disincentives for units to bring out-of-area reserve component members on orders for 180 days or less, even if that member is more qualified for a position than others. As a result, the RegAF might seek to fill open positions with members who reside locally, rather than pay for members to remain on TDY.[46] One senior ANG official also noted specific difficulties for the ANG in using TDY funding to acquire individuals for active-duty positions in distant locations:

> For example, in Fairbanks, Alaska, we needed help with certain exper-
> tise and we could not take on contractors. So we have to look within
> other states to TDY in support, but this comes out of TDY rather than
> PCS and there are barriers with the ANG in doing this. It can differ
> across the 54 states and territories.[47]

Additionally, for members on TDY orders, per diem and housing allowances also change depending on the length of the orders. According to the JTR, different per diem flat rates apply based on the number of days spent on TDY. If a member spends between 31 and 180 days at a single location, then a flat rate of 75 percent of per diem is issued for each full day. If a member extends beyond 181 days while on TDY, then the member receives 55 percent of the per diem for each full day. Members serving less than 30 days receive a full daily per diem. If members' orders change during their time on TDY, then they will receive a new per diem flat rate based on the new total number of days, beginning the day of their adjusted orders. For example, if

---

[45] Interview AF7, ANG official, November 7, 2017.

[46] Interview AF4, senior ANG official, April 11, 2018; DoD, *The Joint Travel Regulations: Uniformed Service Members and DoD Civilian Employees*, July 1, 2018, pp. 3A-4–3A-6. See also Interview AF7, ANG official, November 7, 2017.

[47] Interview AF5, U.S. Air Force senior official, April 11, 2018.

a member accepts orders for 25 days, then receives an extension of orders for 50 more days, the member will receive 55 percent of the per diem flat rate starting the day he or she receive the extension.[48] While these rules apply to all members of the U.S. Air Force, they can make taking TDY tours for over 30 days difficult for reserve component members because the members receive reduced financial assistance. This can be especially problematic for those members who may be repeatedly requested for frequent missions and must TDY to a location outside their own community. At the very least, these different rates cause confusion throughout the U.S. Air Force and DoD. Indeed, the Government Accountability Office released a report in May 2017 recommending that DoD clarify aspects of its per diem policy.[49] While this rule was in effect while conducting this study, Section 603 of the John S. McCain Fiscal Year 2019 National Defense Authorization Act eliminates the use of flat-rate per diem when a traveler is on a TDY assignment at one location for more than 30 days, and the references to this limitation have been removed from the JTR.

Variances in Basic Allowance for Housing Rates

Certain housing allowances also change based on length of order, which can cause difficulties for members to accept shorter-term orders. These constraints most frequently affect reserve component members who take local active-duty orders, as they would not qualify for TDY orders. The JTR states that reserve component members serving in active-duty positions for more than 30 days will receive the basic housing allowance that an active-duty member receives. However, if they serve in a voluntary position for less than 30 days, they receive a housing allowance specific to reserve component members, known as the Basic Allowance for Housing–Reserve Component (BAH-RC), which is typically much lower than the basic allowance for housing rate.[50] Consequently, reserve component members who are

---

[48] DoD, 2018, pp. 2-24–2-44.

[49] U.S. Government Accountability Office, *DoD Joint Travel Regulations Actions Are Needed to Clarify Flat Rate Per Diem Policy*, Washington, D.C., GAO-17-353, May 2017.

[50] DoD, 2018, pp. 10E13-1–10E13-4. The BAH-RC rate is calculated based on the Basic Allowance for Quarters of December 31, 1997, incremented by the average housing allowance increase each year.

asked to conduct a number of short-term tours under the 30-day mark end up receiving less support for housing. Additionally, if a reserve component member has a break in active duty when the member would otherwise perform service for over 30 days, that break in active duty will revert the member's rate back to the reserve component rate. For example, one interviewee stated that if a reserve component member is needed to conduct training for one day, he or she will be hesitant to do so as it breaks the member's orders for that day, resulting in a decrease in the member's overall housing allowance. The official also noted that changes in basic allowance for housing rates are applied for members who take on active-duty orders, which proves detrimental to the member if the changes reduce the allowance.[51] Reductions in housing rates can also be difficult for reserve component members who take orders for educational or career development opportunities. They may be required to move to a different area for these opportunities, and upon return find themselves earning much less in their housing allowance.[52]

Burdensome Waiver Processes

As we note in the AGR, 1,095 man-day, and JTR subsections, waivers may be obtained for the policies described earlier. However, an overall constraint facing reserve component utilization is that these waiver processes tend to create substantial administrative burdens for both service members and units seeking exceptions to policy. Several interviewees reported that waivers serve as barriers to mission completion, noting that the time required to complete the waivers could be better spent working toward their mission's goals, rather than filing requisite paperwork. The burden of completing waivers disproportionately falls on individual units and commanders who often feel pressured to meet other, more important demands with their limited time. One interviewee described the 1,095 man-day waiver process as a "bureaucratic nightmare," while two others believed waiver processes should be removed completely.[53] A senior U.S. Air Force official also pointed out

---

[51] Interview AF3, senior U.S. Air Force officers, April 26, 2018.

[52] Interview AF3, senior U.S. Air Force officers, April 26, 2018.

[53] Interview AF7, ANG official, November 7, 2017; Interview AF5, senior ANG official, April 11, 2018; and Interview AF10, senior U.S. Air Force official, May 31, 2018.

that when a service member is waiting for a waiver to be approved, "that person is of no value as they go through the waiver process, so you lose them during that time."[54]

Permeability Constraints

Permeability refers to the ability of service members to move across the active and reserve components, and is often constrained by bureaucratic and procedural factors. Permeability is considered a valuable retention and talent management tool. The RFPB highlights the importance of permeability by making the following recommendation in their 2016 report:

> Enhance Permeability by Easing Transitions. The Department should encourage transition between the service components and remove the barriers impeding it. A Total Force personnel system should be developed that allows for the seamless transition of service members within DoD (i.e. between the services and their components). Greater permeability will allow service members to transition between the active component and reserve component, retaining valuable talent by providing service members flexibility that accommodates changing life circumstances. Reduction of statutory impediments and bureaucratic administrative requirements should be accomplished to ease these transitions.[55]

Separate Pay and Benefits Systems

A primary challenge in permeability is that ARC and RegAF members do not share the same personnel management, readiness, and pay systems. This creates multiple challenges that disproportionately affect reserve component members. First, errors and delays in pay often occur as members move between RegAF and ARC systems, which could affect reserve component members' willingness to volunteer for active-duty missions. Several officials noted that members may wait several months to receive pay, and

---

[54] Interview AF10, senior U.S. Air Force official, May 31, 2018.

[55] RFPB, 2016, p. 51.

interviewees repeatedly identified delays in pay as a common concern.[56] Delays disproportionately affect reserve component members, whose units may be smaller and have fewer administrative staff members.[57] As one interviewee noted, "The systems underlying pay and benefits are not set up to support ARC members."[58]

Second, members' entitlements, which include health and other benefits, differ based on their component affiliation and the duty status in which they are serving at any time.[59] Senior U.S. Air Force officers described the process in an interview:

> With AGRs, you are on TRICARE, but with military technicians, you are on private insurance; if you are part time, you are switching back and forth. You change statuses for missions, so members end up spending a lot of time switching all of their benefits back and forth. It causes a lot of pain.[60]

In certain instances, reserve component members need to break active-duty orders in order to perform reserve duty, which requires them to restart their entitlements and benefits with each break. One interviewee noted that ANG members are less willing to go on active duty because it might cause problems for their entitlements.

Third, personnel and readiness data for RegAF and ARC members is stored in separate, compartmentalized systems, which makes accessing data across components difficult. One U.S. Air Force official familiar with total force planning stated that active-duty wing commanders do not have access to both ARC Personnel Accounting Symbol codes, which is challenging as the codes denote members' specific units and provide commanders

---

[56] Interview AF3, senior U.S. Air Force officers, April 26, 2018; and Interview AF5, senior ANG official, April 11, 2018.

[57] Interview AF10, senior U.S. Air Force official, May 31, 2018.

[58] Interview AF7, ANG official, November 7, 2017.

[59] Interview AF3, senior U.S. Air Force officers, April 26, 2018; Interview AF4, senior ANG official, April 11, 2018; and Interview AF9, U.S. Air Force personnel official, November 8, 2017.

[60] Interview AF3, senior U.S. Air Force officers, April 26, 2018.

visibility over members' locations.[61] Another interviewee identified constraints placed on commanders and units because of systemic problems they experience with the M4S, Defense Readiness Reporting System, Status of Resources and Training System, and Defense Manpower Data Center. The official stated that data that get fed into the Defense Readiness Reporting System (the cross-service readiness reporting system) is abundant but often poor in quality and uncollaborative, which prevents the U.S. Air Force and DoD more broadly from "getting an accurate sense of readiness."[62]

The continued development of the U.S. Air Force's Integrated Personnel and Pay System should address the concerns just discussed.

Challenges with Reserve Unit Reaffiliation and Career Progression

Another permeability challenge is that ARC members often lose their reserve component unit positions when volunteering for active duty. This is especially difficult for ANG members who are limited to affiliation within their own state.[63] These challenges limit reserve component members' willingness to volunteer for active-duty missions and may deter members from volunteering in the future if not addressed.[64]

Relatedly, several interviewees stressed the negative consequences that taking active-duty assignments can have on a reserve component member's career progression. Often, this is due to a lack of clarity about whether promotions for a reserve component member on active duty should be handled by the active component or the reserve component, and unclear or even subjective measures as to whether reserve component and active component assignments should be given equal weight in promotion considerations.[65] This lack of clarity as to how reserve component members on active-duty

---

[61] Interview AF8, U.S. Air Force official familiar with total force policies, November 9, 2017.

[62] Interview AF5, senior ANG official, April 11, 2018.

[63] Interview AF6, AFR official, February 1, 2018.

[64] Interview AF10, senior U.S. Air Force official, May 31, 2018.

[65] Interview AF9, U.S. Air Force personnel official, November 8, 2017.

orders can be promoted might dissuade members from taking active-duty assignments. One interviewee gave the example of a reserve component member who was sent on a voluntary MPA to fill a critical need in Japan: "He was on three-year orders for this but was going to hit his board for lieutenant colonel during those years. How do we promote him? He isn't active duty, so can't be promoted by them, but he's not really Reserve either."[66]

Reserve component members on other types of active-duty orders face this challenge as well. In the VLPAD program, for example, enlisted National Guard and Reserve members are not able to test for promotion in the ARC while filling a VLPAD billet because they do not have an ARC unit affiliation. While officers are eligible for promotion while serving in VLPAD billets, their time in the VLPAD program is not considered by the board, which can mean the member is less competitive compared with peers who are not serving in these critical-fill positions.[67]

Cumbersome Scrolling Process

We heard from numerous interviewees about how cumbersome the "scrolling" process can be.[68] *Scrolling* is the term used for the processing of original appointment or certain promotions of officers. Some appointments are made by the Secretary of Defense under authorities delegated by the president. Other appointments are made by the president with the advice and consent of the Senate. A *scroll* refers to a list of officers forwarded to the appointing authority for such an appointment. Numerous potential sources of error and delay make scrolling an administratively challenging process. The transition from active to reserve components currently requires a reappointment through this process because of a distinction in Title 10 between regular and reserve appointments. In particular, we heard that it can take a long time to complete the scrolling process—often more than six months—because there are numerous administrative hoops that paperwork must pass through. As such, the current scrolling process serves as a disincentive to transition between the active and reserve components.

---

[66] Interview AF3, senior U.S. Air Force officers, April 26, 2018.

[67] Interview AF6, AFR official, February 1, 2018.

[68] Interview AF15, senior U.S. Air Force leaders, May 15, 2018.

Lack of Cross-Component Understanding

Other factors that challenge the U.S. Air Force's ability to effectively leverage the ARC are cultural in nature, specifically concerning lack of cross-
component knowledge. The RFPB raised concerns that the active component has a less than complete understanding about the reserve component's
capabilities, needs, and mobilization authorities.[69] While total force efforts
are underway to better integrate capabilities and personnel, both components currently have greater familiarity with their own respective roles and
abilities. This natural bias, combined with limited opportunities for members to serve across components, creates a lack of cross-component understanding. Several of our interviewees noted that the RegAF's lack of understanding of the ARC affects integration and usage of ARC members from
the individual to the strategic level.

Some ARC leaders we spoke with felt that many policies and administrative requirements ignore that ARC members are largely a part-time workforce. For example, because of the limited service days per year as compared with the RegAF, ARC members often face tighter time constraints to
complete certain mandatory courses or trainings. One ANG officer told us
that 30 percent of time reserved for OARIT was subsumed by operational
requirements.[70] Others felt that increased operational tempo uniquely over-
burdens ARC members, who are also faced with balancing civilian career
demands with their military careers, and may face challenges in securing
time off from their civilian positions for military orders.[71]

At higher levels, this lack of education can cause broader issues that
hinder ARC utilization. One interviewee noted that the lack of understanding in the RegAF about ARC needs results in the creation of policies that
create barriers.[72] Some of this might be due to a lack of ARC representation
in key fora where decisions affecting the ARC are made. One ARC commander cited an example of a recent wing commanders' conference where
all 30 attendees were from the RegAF, and noted that the RegAF sees both

---

[69] RFPB, 2016, p. 80.

[70] Interview AF5, senior ANG official, April 11, 2018.

[71] Interview AF5, senior ANG official, April 11, 2018.

[72] Interview AF5, senior ANG official, April 11, 2018.

the AFR and the ANG "as a temporary hiring force."[73] The 2014 NCSAF report highlights this need for greater integration not just at periodic events but in key assignments as well, stating, "Increasing Active-Reserve integration of headquarters and units as well as increasing the number of integrated or multi-component ('associate') units will lead directly to improved processes and more effective and efficient employment of the Total Air Force."[74]

Some career fields might feel this lack of cross-component knowledge more acutely than others. For example, in the space field, one interviewee remarked that the RegAF's knowledge of ARC capabilities is inadequate because of limited discussion between the RegAF and ARC space communities. The interviewee continued, "In this mission area, the ARC is an afterthought. Decisions are made either without ARC inputs or the ARC is brought in at the end of the process."[75]

Lack of understanding can also contribute to a lack of trust between the two components. The NCSAF underscores the necessity of trust in integration at all levels, stating, "The bonds of confidence that Airmen have built over more than a decade of service in war make it reasonable to believe that the necessary levels of trust among the components can be achieved and maintained."[76] This type of trust, and the cross-component knowledge that enables it, can be achieved as RegAF and ARC personnel often work side by side in deployed environments. However, some are concerned that this trust will disappear as deployments to combat zones decrease. One senior ARC member told us, "From my own standpoint, when you are in combat overseas, that's the total force; we are all under one commander. When we are on the continent doing training, then we are definitely not a total force. . . . I think we're going to see a loss of total force after the wars die down."[77]

This dearth of understanding also affects perceptions of the difficulty and costs of employing ARC members. These perceptions affect both the

---

[73] Interview AF10, senior U.S. Air Force official, May 31, 2018.

[74] NCSAF, 2014, p. 19.

[75] Interview AF2, U.S. Department of the Air Force space operations commander, January 9, 2018.

[76] NCSAF, 2014, pp. 18–19, 27.

[77] Interview AF10, senior U.S. Air Force official, May 31, 2018.

resourcing of the ARC at the strategic level and the utilization of the ARC across the force, which can discourage RegAF units from employing ARC members. The RFPB expanded on this point in 2016:

> Most notably, a general lack of knowledge regarding reserve component organization, capabilities, policies, access, cost, etc. has led some leaders to believe that the reserve component is not as capable or effective as their active component counterparts and that they cost too much. The continuing failure of DoD to calculate fully-burdened and life-cycle costs of its Active, Guard, Reserve and other categories of personnel is the root cause of most of these problems. These assumptions have proven false after reviewing the actual fully burdened costs of maintaining Active and Reserve forces and the independent analysis of reserve component performance in combat.[78]

One interviewee felt that the ANG is seen as particularly difficult for the RegAF to access, both in terms of the process by which to employ ANG members and in the perception that the ANG is not willing to provide personnel to support RegAF missions even if they could provide necessary platforms.[79] Overall, these misperceptions can extend to the highest levels of government, causing the RFPB to observe, "Lack of knowledge by senior service and DoD leaders leads to common misperceptions about the reserve component which limits effective integration, and inhibits proper use of capabilities and experience."[80]

Lessons from Other Services

To identify potential options for the U.S. Air Force to better access reservists through long-term orders, we briefly analyzed the other military services' efforts toward total force integration and management of reserve component members on active-duty orders. In the following sections, we highlight specific lessons learned from the Army, Navy, and Marine Corps that may

---

[78] RFPB, 2016, pp. 20–21.

[79] Interview AF10, senior U.S. Air Force official, May 31, 2018.

[80] RFPB, 2016, p. 20.

be useful to the U.S. Air Force as options to improve long-term reserve support to the active component.

Army

In the Army, ADOS billets are managed through a skills-to-billet matching system called Tour of Duty. Similar to online civilian employment search sites such as Monster.com, Tour of Duty allows active-duty commands looking for reserve personnel to fill specific billets to create positions; define requirements such as rank, skills, and experiences; and then advertise the positions. Tour of Duty is accessible by any Army soldier. Once logged in, members are able to sort by job type, by military occupational specialty, by location, and more, and are able to apply to multiple positions at one time.

Once a soldier applies to a position and is accepted, the soldier's reserve unit commander is notified, and that commander decides whether to release the member for the active component assignment. If approved, the commander will sign a form that is then routed to the Army's Human Resources Command, which reviews the file to determine readiness for mobilization. Then the file is forwarded to the Army headquarters staff personnel section (G-1), which ensures that the member is not approaching sanctuary and is not in violation of the 1,095 man-day reporting requirement.

According to one interviewee, while Tour of Duty is an effective way to match interested and qualified reserve component members to open billets in the active component, improvements could still be made, specifically in garnering more awareness of the benefits of the system both to units and to reservists. At the same time, greater familiarity with the program could create another problem for the Army: just as in the U.S. Air Force, budget constraints limit how many positions can be opened to reservists, and more visibility could increase demand to a level that the Army could not afford to satisfy.[81]

Navy

The Navy's experience is so different from the U.S. Air Force's that there are few generalizable lessons for the U.S. Air Force. Most important, given

---

[81] Interview AR1, Army G-1 official, June 26, 2018.

the force structure of the Navy, there is little movement between its active component and its Reserve—especially in certain specialties that are wholly concentrated in either the active component or the Navy Reserve. According to our interviewees, the Navy's system of managing reserve members is extremely decentralized, and that decentralization is central to the Navy's culture. As a result, sailors have a great deal of autonomy in moving from assignment to assignment—which sometimes pits the needs of the service against the desires of individuals. However, there is visibility into available assignments, and sailors often feel as if they have greater control over their career progression than in some of the other services.[82]

Marine Corps

The Marine Corps manages reserve members on frequent and long-term active-duty missions through its ADOS program. To fill active-duty positions, the ADOS office sends emails to potential reserve applicants, stating the military occupational specialty and rank needed for specific positions. From the potential pool identified, commanders pull data for qualified individuals to fill their available positions. Because of the small size of the Marine Corps force, the solicitations for reserve members extend nationwide and are not targeted by region. The majority of reserve members go on active-duty orders for mobilizations and thus are attached to their local unit when supporting active missions.

The Marine Corps has a centralized process through their Marine Corps Total Force System for commanders to determine whether members may reach the 1,095 man-day threshold before being put on orders. The function became available for use across the Marine Corps at the end of 2015.[83] The system and process may serve as an example for the U.S. Air Force when streamlining their procedures for waiver exceptions.

To help the active component better access long-term reservists, the Marine Corps ADOS office holds periodic working groups that are open

---

[82] Interview N1, Navy Reserve personnel officials, July 9, 2018.

[83] Marine Administrative Message 469/15, *Procedures Concerning Reserve Marines Serving on Active Duty Operational Support (ADOS) Orders for More Than Three Years Within the Preceding Four-Year Period (1,095 Rule)*, September 24, 2015.

to representatives from each region and command in the Marine Corps, including reserve component and active component, to determine needs across the force. The field sponsors communicate any problems or issues they experience, and the ADOS office works with leadership to implement related changes. According to the Marine Corps official we interviewed, the working group's "focus is to make it easier for our Marines in the field."[84] The U.S. Air Force could consider implementing a similar meeting structure to facilitate the exchange of topics, challenges, and possible solutions among regions and commands that often rely on the reserve component for support. Expanding these meetings to include other services could also provide a forum for sharing best practices in the effective utilization of reserve members across DoD.

In the next chapter, we discuss our recommendations for ways to improve utilization of ARC members for sustained active-duty missions.

---

[84] Interview M1, Marine Corps officials, July 17, 2018.

CHAPTER SIX

Conclusions and Recommendations to Improve Utilization of Air Reserve Component Members for Sustained Active-Duty Missions

In this chapter, we provide conclusions and recommendations to address the legal, resource, policy, and permeability constraints identified in the previous two chapters. The continuing reliance of the RegAF on the ARC since 9/11 has called into question whether current statutes, resource policies, and personnel policies are adequate to address the current utilization of the ARC to support operational missions. Many of these statutes—some dating back to colonial times—were put into place to protect against the overutilization of the reserve components. This includes limits on the duration that reserve component members can serve on active duty and under what conditions they can be called to service. As the ARC has become an operational reserve that provides sustained support to the RegAF, the restrictions associated with these statutes sometimes come into tension with current operational demands on the ARC and the historical priority to protect against overutilization of the reserve component.

This study set out to identify current constraints to the utilization of the ARC for sustained active-duty operational missions and provide recommendations to address those constraints. What we discovered during the course of our discussions with senior U.S. Air Force leaders is that the enduring philosophical debate about the purpose and appropriate utilization of the reserve components continues. Some individuals we spoke with felt passionate that sustained, long-term, or frequent operational support to the RegAF is an appropriate use of the ARC, while others expressed concern that, in their view, the ARC was never intended to provide such long-term operational support to the RegAF, and that such sustained operations could have negative impacts on recruiting, retention, and morale in the ARC. Yet others expressed resignation that the ARC has to find ways to continue to provide sustained support because there is no choice—the RegAF currently does not have the required assets (personnel or equipment) to carry out some operational missions on its own.[1] As one interviewee said about the often unclear and ambiguous processes associated with the evolution toward frequent or long-term use of the ARC for active-duty missions, "We're building the plane as we're flying it."[2]

While the U.S. Air Force continues to have this healthy philosophical debate about the purpose and utilization of the ARC, we have outlined the recommendations summarized in Table 6.1 as steps that can be taken to address some of the current pain points that are felt at different levels of the U.S. Air Force as commanders and senior leaders access and utilize ARC members for sustained active-duty operational support missions. Our recommendations address the main constraints that we found in our legal and policy reviews and that our interviewees identified as particular problems associated with providing ARC support to the RegAF for sustained active-duty operational missions. Several of those constraints relate to processes that are problematic and that will need medium- to long-term solutions to address them; however, we found that other constraints are simply caused by ambiguous policies that cause confusion and perpetuate misperceptions about the policies. The U.S. Air Force can address these concerns in the short term by issuing clarifying guidance on those policies.

During our conversations with some of the most senior U.S. Air Force leaders familiar with the U.S. Air Force's strategic planning process, many also described their perspectives regarding broader questions about the role of the ARC in the total force, which included the lack of strategic planning for the ARC and the lack of deliberate planning processes for employment of

---

[1] The shift to an operational reserve was at least partially a choice among alternatives. One way to address current shortfalls in active component capabilities would be to shift some force structure from the reserve component to the active component.

[2] Interview AF5, senior ANG official, April 11, 2018.

the ARC for sustained support to the RegAF. These issues arose more generally as perceived constraints to the strategic utilization of the ARC and the U.S. Air Force's ability to carry out the Total Force Policy.

Many of these questions are part of the broader philosophical debate about the purpose and utilization of the ARC moving forward. For instance, several interviewees lamented that the ARC's role is often not included in strategic planning at the highest levels and therefore the ARC is left "reverse engineering" policies and strategies that flow down from higher levels. This can lead to confusion about the U.S. Air Force's vision for its ARC and its role in the total force, as well as ad hoc development of policies and processes, and subsequent ad hoc workarounds to those policies and processes. Many of our interviewees suggested that the U.S. Air Force try to more accurately assess manpower requirements for operational support and then fund them accordingly. Our recommendation to realign the current strength accounting requirement away from individual ARC members to the organizations requesting such support is one step toward better assessing the requirement or demand signal for ARC support.

In addition to our recommendations outlined in the previous chapter, we also offer the following bigger-picture recommendations to address broader concerns that senior leaders and commanders raised to us. While we have not formally evaluated these perspectives and concerns, we include them and associated recommendations because they were raised by a critical mass of senior leaders we spoke with. These recommendations include the following:

- Further clarify the U.S. Air Force's vision for the ARC and its role in the total force.
- Tie the U.S. Air Force's vision for the ARC and ARC inputs into strategic planning processes.
- Total force issues (e.g., force structure, employment of the ARC) should flow down from this strategic vision through a deliberate planning process.

A summary of the constraints that we identified as a result of our analyses can be found in Table 6.1.

Given that the U.S. Air Force has been consumed with enduring conflicts since 9/11 and it appears that continuing need for ARC support to

TABLE 6.1

Summary of Constraints to Air Reserve Component Utilization and Recommendations to Address Them

Constraints to ARC Utilization	Recommendations
Strategic	
Uncertainty over the U.S. Air Force's vision of the appropriate role and use of the ARC for sustained operational support missions	Further clarify the U.S. Air Force's vision for the ARC and its role in the total force
Lack of ARC input into strategic planning processes for employment of the ARC for sustained operational support missions	Tie the U.S. Air Force's vision for the ARC and ARC inputs into strategic planning processes
Lack of a deliberate planning process for employment of the ARC for sustained operational support missions	Total force issues (e.g., force structure, employment of the ARC) should flow down from this strategic vision through a deliberate planning process
Legal	
Duty status system	Continue to support duty status reform
Legal structure that dictates rigid funding streams for components	Enable some budget flexibility
Potential constraints placed on volunteerism by current 1,095 man-day strength accounting requirement	Realign the strength accounting requirement
Limitations on duties that FTS personnel may perform	Address the limitations placed on FTS personnel
Resource	
Lack of adequate and predictable funding	Program sufficient operational support funding for the ARC
Volatility added to budget-planning process by CRs	Stress to lawmakers the toll that CRs have on the U.S. Air Force
Funding disconnected from end strength	Align appropriations with strength accounting
Rigidity of resource management processes	Enable some budget flexibility
Policy	
Ambiguous FTS personnel policies	Clarify ambiguous policies
Confusion over 1,095 man-day rule	Clarify ambiguous policies
Lack of clarity and flexibility on JTR	Provide clarity and flexibility in travel and housing allowances
Burdensome waiver processes	Reduce waiver requirements

Table 6.1—Continued

Constraints to ARC Utilization	Recommendations
Permeability	
Separate pay and benefits systems	Continue to support development of the U.S. Air Force's Integrated Personnel and Pay System
Challenges with reserve unit reaffiliation and career progression	Enable ARC members' career progression while on active duty
Cumbersome scrolling process	Streamline or eliminate the scrolling process
Lack of cross-component understanding	Facilitate cross-component experiences

the RegAF will not wane anytime soon, this may be a good time for the U.S. Air Force to revisit the ongoing dialogue about the purpose and appropriate employment of its ARC—especially with regard to sustained operational support to the RegAF. While attention often focuses on the day-to-day constraints to utilizing the ARC that we discuss in this report (e.g., 1,095 man-day waivers and travel allowances), the crux of debates surrounding these types of constraints stems from larger questions about appropriate employment of the ARC. The recommendations provided in this report aim to provide the U.S. Air Force with options for addressing various levels of constraints to ARC utilization for sustained operational support missions. We discuss each of these recommendations next.

Recommendations to Address Legal Constraints

There are four broad areas that appear to be of the greatest concern and that would require legislative relief:

- the complexities of the current duty status system
- the legal structure that dictates rigid funding streams for each component
- the end-strength accounting requirement for reserve component members performing operational support—orders specifying a period

greater than three years or the cumulative period of active duty that exceeds 1,095 man-days out of the previous 1,460 days
- the limitations placed on FTS personnel (AGRs and military technicians).

The following recommendations include specific legislative changes the U.S. Air Force might consider to minimize the legal constraints on the employment of the ARC to support RegAF missions.

Continue to Support Duty Status Reform

Duty status reform, with the attributes specified by Congress, provides opportunities to address a number of the problems with the current system. Pay and benefits can be aligned with the duty performed. This will ensure all members performing duty in each category receive the same pay and benefit package. Further, volunteers and members involuntarily ordered to duty can serve under the same authority, which will eliminate the differences in pay and benefits that are now dependent on whether the member serves voluntarily or involuntarily. This type of system will allow for better alignment of the planning, programming, budgeting, and execution process with the duty being performed.

Depending on how duty status reform legislation is drafted and what Congress might enact, many of the limitations the U.S. Air Force is currently experiencing might be resolved, or at least minimized, with comprehensive reform to the current duty status construct.

Enable Some Budget Flexibility

While the MPA, RPA, and NGPA funding streams are separate and delineated by different purposes, the U.S. Air Force could explore other ways to fund operational support missions—including programming for it in the POM process. Alternatively, it could alleviate the mismatch between the ARC providing the manpower and the RegAF providing the funding for these types of missions. It could do so by allocating a certain amount of funding to the ARC itself to carry out operational support missions. Some of these options may need congressional approval to implement, but if the U.S. Air Force decides that it is not enough to improve the current MPA,

RPA, and NGPA funding processes, these alternatives may provide the flexibility the U.S. Air Force needs to fund ARC support in multiple ways.

Realign the Strength Accounting Requirement

Rather than hold individual service members accountable for the number of days they are on active duty providing operational support, we recommend realigning the requirement to instead hold commands accountable for the number of days they are provided operational support by reserve component personnel. This data can be tracked through the M4S. Members would continue to receive credit for the duty they performed just as they do today but would not be subject to the strength accounting requirement under the current 1,095 rule. Tracking command utilization rather than individual utilization will unmask structural shortfalls, whereas tracking individual utilization simply identifies those members who are routinely available to meet manpower demand but does not shed any light on where there are demands that cannot be met with active-duty personnel.

To properly account for and document manpower requirements, the operational support strength accounting requirement should be redirected to require commands that continuously rely on reserve component members in order to meet active operational missions to request a waiver when reserve manpower utilization exceeds an established threshold. The thresholds currently established for strength accounting could be used for this purpose. In other words, lift the 1,095 man-day accounting requirement for the member (the supply side) and place it on the command (the demand side). While it may be more challenging to track command utilization of reserve component members if commands disguise the requirement by changing its description, if a command continues to request reserve component personnel for the same general purpose or request personnel of a particular grade or specialty, it should become clear that this is more than a temporary bridge to meet a short-term or emerging mission requirement.

Address the Limitations Placed on Full-Time Support Personnel

Since the utilization of FTS personnel is particularly constrained by the perception that a majority of their time must be spent on their primary responsibilities (OARIT for AGRs and OAIT for military technicians), addressing these perceived limitations is key. There are several approaches that could be pursued to enable AGRs and military technicians to support active component missions more:

- Assign specific operational support missions as an additional duty that FTS personnel may perform. This can be accomplished under the 2006 amendment to current law. However, the restrictions in law (i.e., the "not to interfere with" clause) on the primary duties of AGRs remain applicable and limit the availability of AGRs and military technicians.
- Amend the sections of law that prescribe the primary duties for AGRs and military technicians to include the phrase "or other duties authorized by the Secretary concerned." Alternatively, as suggested the Office of the Air Force Judge Advocate General, strike the restrictions in law (i.e., the "not to interfere with" clause) on the primary duties of AGRs. Either approach would provide the secretary of the U.S. Air Force (and the other service secretaries) with greater flexibility to employ FTS personnel to support assigned missions.
- A much more radical approach would be to merge active guard and reserve and operational support into a single category. The authorized AGR strength and the strength ceiling for operational support would be combined for a total strength for support personnel. Such a merger could address many of the concerns identified individually with each category. The strength accounting requirement for operational support could be eliminated, thus precluding the need for a waiver. And those previously in the active guard and reserve personnel category could perform any mission or duty authorized by the secretary of the U.S. Air Force.
- As members of the Selected Reserve, military technicians can be ordered to active duty or FTNG duty (for Title 32 military technicians), and once on active duty or FTNG duty, they could perform any support mission as a TR or DSG. Duty status reform, described later in this chapter, might make this a more attractive option.

Without a significant philosophical change to the original purpose of FTS personnel, the second and third approaches will be extremely difficult to achieve. Recent evidence of this was Congress's response to the 2015 U.S. Air Force legislative proposed to expand the primary duties of FTS personnel to include instructing or training members of the armed forces on active duty or members of foreign military forces.[3] Congress did not support a permanent expansion of duties but did provide temporary relief during FY 2016 by authorizing not more than 50 FTS personnel to provide pilot training to members on active duty and foreign military member who are in the United States. Congress also directed the secretary of the U.S. Air Force to submit a report to Congress with a plan to eliminate shortages in instructor pilots using authorities available under current law.[4] In 2017, Congress granted a one-year extension of this temporary authority.[5] But it is clear that in 2006 and again in 2015, Congress was not receptive to infringing on or otherwise expanding the primary duties of FTS personnel.

A very strong case would have to be presented to Congress to achieve this type of reform. Even given the fact that Congress has supported other reform initiatives, such as consolidation of special and incentive pays, consolidation and reform of the travel and transportation authorities, the new blended retirement system, and more recently duty status reform, convincing it that this type of reform is necessary to an operational reserve will be challenging.

Recommendations to Address Resource Constraints

While much of what constrains the U.S. Air Force's budget may be out of its control, including the fundamentally challenging impact that CRs have on budget predictability, certain steps can be taken to mitigate the toll these funding challenges take on the reserve components.

---

[3] Department of Defense Office of Legislative Counsel, Sixth Package of Legislative Proposals Sent to Congress for Inclusion in the National Defense Authorization Act for Fiscal Year 2016, Sent to Congress on April 10, 2015 [Sec. 517. Expansion of Authorized Primary Duties of Air Force Reserve Component Full-Time Support Personnel].

[4] Public Law 114-92, National Defense Authorization Act for Fiscal Year 2016, Section 514, November 25, 2015, 129 Stat. 809.

[5] Public Law 114-328, National Defense Authorization Act for Fiscal Year 2017, Section 515, December 23, 2016, 130 Stat. 2113.

Program Sufficient Operational Support Funding for the Reserve Components

Within its POM, the U.S. Air Force can more strictly set aside funding for ARC operational support (for both voluntary and involuntary mobilizations under U.S.C. Title 10, Section 12304b) to RegAF missions and actively limit transfers of these funds to other priorities. This fencing would help ARC units to more accurately plan how they will source support to the RegAF and also fulfill their own requirements without having to constantly be forced to react to reallocations. The U.S. Air Force can also deliberately forecast and plan for its reliance on ARC operational support in the POM. The fencing of funds specifically for operational support will not necessarily entail an increase in costs to the ARC, but increased funding would help to offset the trade-offs between other ARC requirements and ARC support for operational missions.

Continue to Stress to Lawmakers the Toll That Continuing Resolutions Have on the U.S. Air Force

Although the U.S. Air Force's role in federal budget legislation is limited, it can continue to convey the full range of implications that such piecemeal funding has on both the active component and the reserve components. Evidence of how this type of budgeting affects individual service members, readiness of the force, and operational capabilities should be captured and relayed to lawmakers so they are informed of the repercussions CRs have.

Align Appropriations with Strength Accounting

Align appropriations with strength authorization by authorizing an appropriate funding level of NGPA and RPA to correspond to the number of reserve personnel authorized to be on active duty for operational support. This would place the source for both the manpower and funding in the hands of the commander tasked with filling the requirement—the director of the ANG and chief of the AFR.

Enable Some Budget Process Flexibility

To mitigate challenges posed by the rigid budgeting system as it relates to ARC utilization, the U.S. Air Force could take a number of steps. First, it could revisit its process of issuing funding for orders on a quarterly basis, which creates barriers for longer-term orders. Greater latitude to fund orders throughout the fiscal year—and across fiscal year boundaries—could provide the flexibility needed to recruit and retain the right reserve personnel, and provide adequate time to notify their civilian employers of their upcoming duty. Aligning orders with funding availability could also help ensure that ARC members receive their full benefits based on the entire length of commitment, rather than on multiple shorter orders that must be used under the current system.

Some budgeting flexibility could also be pursued in increasing the responsibility and autonomy the ARC has in managing funds. One possibility could be creating a fund that the ARC manages to support operational missions for CCMDs and the RegAF.

Recommendations to Address Policy Constraints

Through our research we identified U.S. Air Force policies that constrained the effective utilization of the ARC for active-duty missions. This section offers options to consider in addressing the challenges posed by these policies.

Clarify Ambiguous Policies

As identified in Chapter Five, unclear and ambiguous policies can lead to difficulties in accessing the ARC for active-duty missions. Misconceptions over the use of AGRs, the 1,095 man-day reporting requirement, and the application of federal travel policy inhibit the use of ARC members. By clarifying these policies, the U.S. Air Force can ameliorate some of the limitations that these misconceptions create. In fact, several of our interviewees specifically stated that guidance clarifying the 1,095 man-day reporting requirement would be useful.

One method for clarifying policies could be through the revision or issuance of policy documents (e.g., DoD directives and instructions) that specifically address the policies at hand, to include direction on the areas of misinterpretation highlighted in Chapter Five. For example, distributing an instructive memorandum on the appropriate proportion of time AGRs may devote to OARIT responsibilities would help to ensure that AGRs can perform duties related to active missions at the level needed and not be limited to an arbitrary percentage of time not included within law or policy. A memorandum on the 1,095 man-day reporting requirement could clarify that the requirement is only for reporting and should not be viewed as a limit to active-duty service. A clarifying memorandum on the application of federal travel policy could provide common examples of travel experiences, such as switching from PCS to TDY, so that members more consistently interpret the federal guidelines.

Provide Flexibility in Travel and Housing Allowances

Certain policies, such as requiring a PCS for orders longer than 180 days, appear to limit which members units are able to bring on orders, because some members are unwilling or unable to move to a new location for an assignment. The U.S. Air Force could amend policy to provide commanders more flexibility to determine when situations warrant an exception to the 180-day rule for transition from TDY to PCS benefits. Granting commanders the ability to continue TDY allowances over 180 days in warranted cases could reduce the limitations currently imposed by these policies.

Depending on the details of the policy change and the extent to which waivers would be administered to provide TDY allowances for orders longer than 180 days, this could result in a fairly large increase in costs in the form of additional per diem payouts. All orders greater than 180 days would potentially become eligible for TDY allowances that could balloon travel budgets. However, some of these costs would be offset by decreases in relocation assistance provided by PCS orders. If the use of this policy is fairly limited and on a case-by-case basis, the cost impact would likely be relatively small.

Additionally, members may be less willing to take on shorter-term orders as a result of their decrease in housing allowances because of the rate change for orders of 30 days or less. Changing the law and policy to allow commanders some flexibility in offering full housing allowance rates for shorter-term orders provides them with an incentive to acquire qualified individuals for short-term tours. If this barrier were addressed, reserve component members may also take opportunities for career development and education more frequently.

Similar to the potential cost impacts associated with allowing TDY allowances for orders greater than 180 days, the cost impact to the U.S. Air Force of allowing members to receive the Basic Allowance for Housing–Active Component (BAH-AC) rather than the BAH-RC depends on the frequency with which commanders administer such waivers. Currently, the average delta between the BAH-AC and the BAH-RC is approximately $650–$750 per month depending on pay grade and whether the member has dependents. If the usage of such a policy change is on a case-by-case basis, and given that this policy change would be for orders less than 30 days, meaning the per-month delta between the BAH-AC and the BAH-RC would be prorated, the anticipated cost impact would likely be relatively small.

Reduce Waiver Requirements

To reduce the administrative burden of waiver application processes, the U.S. Air Force could consider simplifying the waiver process by delegating certain waiver approvals to a lower level of command than currently stated in policy. This could reduce the time needed for the waiver process, as decisions about exceptions could be made more easily and quickly by lower-level commanders with fewer demands on their time than their superiors.

Further, the U.S. Air Force could consider whether to eliminate certain waiver requirements, such as for the 1,095 man-day rule. As stated previously, reserve component members are not restricted from serving more than 1,095 man-days in a 1,460 man-day period; they simply need to be counted toward active-duty end strength. The waivers for this policy currently serve primarily as an accounting mechanism to keep track of reserve component members who are in this situation, but a more efficient process could be to eliminate the waivers and instead adopt more transparent and standardized data collection across components, as recommended in the following section.

As with any process, simplifying the process or using less expensive labor (i.e., lower level of command) will lead to cost savings. The exact savings would be difficult to quantify, but there would likely be marginal savings to the U.S. Air Force if it took one or both of the recommended actions.

Recommendations to Address Permeability Constraints

Continue to Support Development of the Air Force's Integrated Personnel and Pay System

As described in Chapter Five, many reserve component members experience difficulties with receiving pay and benefits when transferring to active duty and back to the reserve components, and separately stored personnel and readiness data inhibit ARC utilization at the unit and enterprise levels. The U.S. Air Force should continue to integrate these systems across the RegAF and ARC, and standardize data collection across components as well. The recognition of the inadequacy of the current system and the recommendation for an improvement is not new. The NCSAF's 2014 report underscored the incongruent nature of the service's system and recommended that the U.S. Air Force accelerate its development of an integrated pay and personnel system that accounts for all three components.[6] The RFPB also emphasized the same recommendation in its 2016 report.[7]

Overall, an integrated system should be aligned with the current operational nature of the ARC.[8] This type of integration would create two primary benefits. First, accelerating efforts to integrate systems that manage pay and benefits across the RegAF and the ARC into one streamlined system would afford the U.S. Air Force the means to enhance management of long-term ARC members and enable greater permeability between the RegAF and ARC. Such an integrated system could improve efficiency and effectiveness of the provision of pay and benefits, both for units and for individual members.

Second, such an integrated system could serve as a data repository for accurate accounting of members' time in both active and reserve statuses and for readiness reporting data, and it could ultimately help to mitigate gaps in assessing an individual's or unit's ability to mobilize. As noted previously, U.S. Air Force officials face challenges in the quality of, and access to,

---

[6] NCSAF, 2014, pp. 50–51.

[7] RFPB, 2016, p. 51.

[8] Interview AF3, senior U.S. Air Force officers, April 26, 2018, p. 5; Interview AF5, senior ANG official, April 11, 2018; and Interview AF8, U.S. Air Force official familiar with total force policies, November 9, 2017.

data for personnel records and readiness across components. Further, ARC members struggle to maintain a true accounting of their active federal service under current policies and procedures. Standardizing and simplifying such methods of data collection across components can assist the U.S. Air Force in easing the transition of reserve members serving on active duty.

Enable Air Reserve Component Members' Career Progression While on Active Duty

To enable enlisted ARC members to test for promotion while on active-duty tours, the U.S. Air Force should assign the members administrative reserve units that are responsible for their promotion review when filling an active-duty assignment. More broadly, the secretary of the U.S. Air Force can provide guidance to promotion boards to assign promotion points for cross-component career-broadening experiences. Further, U.S. Air Force leadership can clarify the policies and procedures that govern promotion processes as they apply to reserve members when they are on active duty.

Streamline or Eliminate the Scrolling Process

We heard from numerous interviewees about how cumbersome the scrolling process can be.[9] In particular, it can take a long time and there are numerous administrative hoops that paperwork must pass through. There are multiple efforts and proposals underway to streamline or eliminate the scrolling process.[10] Our recommendation is that the U.S. Air Force continue to support those efforts.

---

[9] *Scrolling* is the term used for the processing of original appointment or certain promotions of officers. Some appointments are made by the secretary of defense under authorities delegated by the president. Other appointments are made by the president with the advice and consent of the Senate. A *scroll* is a list of officers forwarded to the appointing authority for such an appointment. Numerous potential sources of error and delay make scrolling an administratively challenging process. The transition from active to reserve components currently requires a reappointment through this process due to a distinction in Title 10 between regular and reserve appointments.

[10] The services have sought legislative relief from the distinction in Title 10 between regular and reserve appointments, which has been found by the services to sometimes delay movement between components. Section 501 of the FY 2020 National Defense Authorization Act requires a report on the feasibility of removing this distinction, thereby permitting movement between components without reappointment.

Facilitate Cross-Component Experiences

Efforts to facilitate the utilization of the ARC could be enhanced by facilitating cross-component experiences in which members of the ARC and RegAF spend time exposed to the culture and capabilities in multiple components. These could include cross-component assignments in which active component personnel are assigned to reserve component units, or reserve component personnel are assigned to active component units. Such experiences would help service members to better understand the needs and capabilities of the active and reserve components and could contribute to greater efficiencies in utilizing reserve component members and in integrating missions. Such an approach could also help to grow leaders who understand all of the components of the U.S. Air Force.[11]

The U.S. Air Force should also focus on the importance of staff and organizational integration at every level as allowed by law. This is another key way in which the U.S. Air Force could build cross-component synergy, break down stovepipes to truly operationalize the ARC in all functions, and build the trust between the components.[12] Congress could also require increased integration or cross-component experiences through its annual authorization bill by establishing minimums for ARC personnel in specific missions and mandating certain headquarters or command positions to be filled by ARC members. This recommendation also falls in line with the NCSAF recommendation on staff integration: "The Air Force should integrate the existing staffs of the Headquarters Air Force, the AFR, and ANG, similar to the principles recommended by the Total Force Task Force."[13]

---

[11] See Agnes Gereben Schaefer, John D. Winkler, Kimberly Jackson, Daniel Ibarra, Darrell D. Jones, and Geoffrey McGovern, *Approaches to Strengthening Total Force Culture and Facilitating Cross-Component Integration in the U.S. Military*, Santa Monica, Calif.: RAND Corporation, RR-2143-OSD, 2020.

[12] See Laurinda L. Rohn, Agnes Gereben Schaefer, Gregory A. Schumacher, Jennifer Kavanagh, Caroline Baxter, and Amy Grace Donohue, *Integrating Active and Reserve Component Staff Organizations: Improving the Chances of Success*, Santa Monica, Calif.: RAND Corporation, RR-1869-OSD, 2019.

[13] NCSAF, 2014, p. 33.

Total Requested Man-Days by Air Force Specialty Code in Fiscal Year 2018

Tables A.1 and A.2 provide the total days requested and approved for all enlisted and officer AFSCs in FY 2018. AFSCs are listed in order of most requested to least requested by request count.

TABLE A.1

Total Requested Enlisted Man-Days by Air Force Specialty Code, Fiscal Year 2018

AFSC	AFSC Title	Days Requested	Days Approved	Request Count
1N0XX	Operations Intelligence	368,914	57,441	220
3D0XX	Knowledge Operations Management	165,891	58,601	211
3S0XX	Personnel	94,129	27,938	178
3D1XX	Client Systems	248,489	78,967	168
3P0XX	Security Forces	169,346	82,624	150
2A5XX	Aerospace Maintenance	336,573	69,398	110
1N4XX	Network Intelligence Analyst	112,781	38,163	96
1N1XX	Geospatial Intelligence	177,587	48,335	93
4N0XX	Aerospace Medical Service	86,512	38,180	92
3A1XX	Information Management	31,503	11,838	91
2A3XX	Avionics Systems	3,626,465	326,065	87

Table A.1—Continued

AFSC	AFSC Title	Days Requested	Days Approved	Request Count
1A9XX	Special Missions Aviation	29,413	19,542	73
5R0XX	Chaplain Assistant	21,698	7,635	73
1A2XX	Aircraft Loadmaster	136,902	38,624	71
3E0XX	Electrical Systems	20,564	5,971	59
1C3XX	Command Post	18,966	9,590	57
1A1XX	Flight Engineer	126,956	30,394	56
2G0XX	Logistics Plans	13,003	4,790	47
4A0XX	Health Services Management	8,316	3,644	46
6F0XX	Financial Management and Comptroller	28,361	6,058	45
1C6XX	Space Systems Operations	35,252	11,801	41
1N2XX	Signals Intelligence Analyst	27,564	9,512	40
2S0XX	Materiel Management	29,021	6,237	40
2T2XX	Air Transportation	235,786	3,107	35
1B4XX	Cyberspace Defense Operations	58,760	25,414	34
1N3XX	Cryptologic Language Analyst	37,747	18,147	34
3M0XX	Services	17,154	4,907	33
1A0XX	In-Flight Refueling	35,655	17,426	32
1C0XX	Aviation Resource Management	14,564	6,568	32
2A6XX	Aerospace Propulsion	24,259	10,251	32
1P0XX	Aircrew Flight Equipment	10,483	6,168	30
2A0XX	Avionics Test Station and Components	117,353	52,810	29
2T0XX	Traffic Management	12,790	6,836	29
1A8XX	Airborne Cryptologic Linguist	28,744	18,461	28
1W0XX	Weather	36,883	12,737	27
1T2XX	Pararescue	5,214	1,744	25
3E7XX	Fire Protection	17,049	1,751	23

Table A.1—Continued

AFSC	AFSC Title	Days Requested	Days Approved	Request Count
3F0XX	Personnel	5,310	0	23
1C5XX	Command and Control Battle Manager	8,377	1,975	22
2T3XX	Vehicle Maintenance	5,045	1,245	22
3N0XX	Public Affairs	3,996	810	20
2A8XX	Aerospace Maintenance	30,369	7,222	19
3E2XX	Pavement and Construction Equipment	22,668	3,127	18
1U0XX	Career RPA Sensor Operator	201,967	68,149	17
3E5XX	Engineering	8,553	326	17
3S2XX	Education and Training	5,367	1,668	17
6C0XX	Contracting	2,407	989	17
2A7XX	Aircraft Metals Technology	28,467	21,668	16
3E6XX	Operations Management	3,832	1,238	16
3E9XX	Emergency Management	7,290	466	16
4Y0XX	Dental Assistant	1,512	1,038	16
3E1XX	HVAC	6,230	1,659	14
3E3XX	Structural	7,846	2,800	14
3E8XX	Explosive Ordnance Disposal	6,551	927	14
2W0XX	Munitions Systems	5,016	1,870	13
2F0XX	Fuels	3,532	2,696	12
2T1XX	Vehicle Operations	8,122	1,498	11
2W1XX	Aircraft Armament Systems	6,369	678	10
1S0XX	Safety	2,572	1,301	9
3E4XX	Water and Fuel Systems Maintenance	3,425	1,025	8
5J0XX	Paralegal	13,581	8,766	8
9S1XX	Scientific Applications Specialist	4,327	183	8

Table A.1—Continued

AFSC	AFSC Title	Days Requested	Days Approved	Request Count
1C2XX	Combat Control	3,871	2,230	6
2R0XX	Maintenance Management Analysis	13,212	626	6
3F2XX	Career Field Manager	892	0	6
4A1XX	Medical Material	180	179	6
4C0XX	Mental Health Service	1,916	1,102	6
7S0XX	Special Investigations	6,630	6,630	6
8A3XX	Career Assistant Advisor	2,138	336	6
8I0XX	Wing Inspections Superintendent	1,197	810	6
1C7XX	Airfield Management	1,840	1	5
2A2XX	Aerospace Maintenance	1,761	1,139	5
3F1XX	Services	1,390	0	5
3F5XX	Administrative Support	721	180	5
3S1XX	Equal Opportunity	1,174	720	5
4B0XX	Bioenvironmental Engineering	513	230	5
8B0XX	Military Training Instructor	5,424	4,135	5
9G1XX	Group Superintendent	1,690	0	5
1A3XX	Airborne Mission System	1,377	1,047	4
1B0XX	Knowledge/Cyber System Operations	960	948	4
1C1XX	Air Traffic Control	860	183	4
1C4XX	Tactical Air Control Party	2,238	1,500	4
1C8XX	Airfield Systems	4,000	0	4
1N7XX	Human Intelligence	122	0	4
2A9XX	Aerospace Maintenance	2,030	380	4
4P0XX	Pharmacy	722	1	4
4T0XX	Medical Laboratory	22	42	4
3N1XX	Regional Band	151	120	3
3S3XX	Manpower	929	180	3

Table A.1—Continued

AFSC	AFSC Title	Days Requested	Days Approved	Request Count
4A2XX	Biomedical Equipment	214	90	3
4J0XX	Physical Medicine	1,112	30	3
4N1XX	Surgical Service	328	28	3
8T0XX	Professional Military Education Instructor	1,620	1,224	3
1T0XX	Survival, Evasion, Resistance and Escape	599	357	2
3F4XX	Personnel	479	0	2
4E0XX	Public Health	11	10	2
4H0XX	Cardiopulmonary Laboratory	360	0	2
4M0XX	Aerospace and Operational Psychology	464	231	2
4V0XX	Ophthalmic	395	30	2
8B2XX	Academy Military Training Noncommissioned Officer	330	330	2
8F0XX	First Sergeant	5,830	2,598	2
8G0XX	Honor Guard	343	231	2
9R0XX	Civil Air Patrol	23,481	23,193	2
1A6XX	Flight Attendant	1,200	1,200	1
2R1XX	Maintenance Management Production	120	0	1
4R0XX	Diagnostic Imaging	60	60	1
8B1XX	Military Training Leader	4,380	4,380	1
8P0XX	Courier	360	252	1
8U0XX	Unit Deployment Manager	150	0	1
9T2XX	Pre-Cadet Assignee	1	0	1
9U1XX	Unidentified	5,010,524	2,120,594	438
Total		12,086,659	3,561,446	3,556

SOURCE: Beast table in M4S data set.

TABLE A.2

Total Requested Officer Man-Days by Air Force Specialty Code, Fiscal Year 2018

AFSC	AFSC Title	Days Requested	Days Approved	Request Count
14N	Intelligence	270,716	48,115	444
11M	Mobility Pilot	368,361	114,780	237
17D	Cyberspace Operations Commander	79,044	28,852	233
16G	Air Force Special Operations Staff Officer	79,424	27,916	228
11F	Fighter Pilot	537,390	112,814	196
62E	Developmental Engineer	13,152	6,766	133
16R	Planning and Programming	30,955	14,706	121
32E	Civil Engineer	23,929	7,445	119
38P	Personnel Officer	38,601	15,713	113
90G	General Officer	18,542	8,825	113
13S	Space Operations	35,544	17,639	113
21R	Logistics Readiness	26,778	11,089	110
11S	Special Operations Pilot	38,339	32,118	107
63A	Acquisition Manager	11,965	3,790	93
11G	Generalist Pilot	21,139	8,931	85
52R	Chaplain	28,512	10,398	82
41A	Health Services Administrator	10,609	2,791	68
21A	Aircraft Maintenance	188,492	14,108	63
46N	Clinical Nurse	8,663	3,109	60
13B	Air Battle Manager	16,069	3,693	56
31P	Security Forces	10,390	2,515	54
64P	Contracting	8,709	8,709	49
35P	Public Affairs	7,156	3,766	47
17S	Cyber Warfare Operations	23,983	8,683	40
65F	Financial Manager	6,923	6,923	36
12M	Mobility Combat Systems Officer	73,321	9,891	33
12S	Special Operations Combat Systems Officer	9,346	6,430	33

Table A.2—Continued

AFSC	AFSC Title	Days Requested	Days Approved	Request Count
44F	Family Physician	2,420	1,012	32
11B	Bomber Pilot	10,954	7,636	25
48R	Residency Trained Flight Surgeon	12,201	5,729	25
81T	Instructor	23,633	15,930	25
11K	Trainer Pilot	36,267	23,324	24
16P	Political-Military Affairs Strategist	6,406	1,126	24
48G	General Medical Officer, Flight Surgeon	15,885	5,782	24
38F	Force Support	4,582	0	22
11U	Remotely Piloted Aircraft Pilot	245,232	85,134	21
51J	Judge Advocate	22,565	13,832	21
61A	Operations Research Analyst	3,319	1,290	21
15W	Weather	2,921	330	19
11H	Rescue Pilot	2,780	976	18
46F	Flight Nurse	7,216	2,425	15
16F	Regional Affairs Strategist	2,927	705	14
12R	Intelligence, Surveillance, and Reconnaissance Combat Systems Officer	2,893	1,622	12
47G	Dentist	448	268	12
11R	Reconnaissance/Surveillance/Electronic Warfare	12,573	8,623	11
12G	Generalist Combat Systems Officer	3,667	2,365	10
13N	Nuclear and Missile Operations	1,226	504	10
13M	Airfield Operations	1,959	744	9
42S	Clinical Social Worker	1,294	730	9
12B	Bomber Combat Systems Officer	1,716	290	8
13D	Combat Rescue Officer	1,570	1,325	8
21M	Munitions and Missile Maintenance	1,355	411	8
97E	Executive Officer	2,030	240	8
18G	Generalist Remotely Piloted Aircraft Pilot	1,608	631	7

Table A.2—Continued

AFSC	AFSC Title	Days Requested	Days Approved	Request Count
43H	Public Health Officer	615	595	7
46Y	Advanced Practice Registered Nurse	1,159	90	7
86M	Operations Management	3,114	1,625	7
87G	Wing Inspector General	786	256	7
42P	Clinical Psychologist	828	828	6
45S	Dermatologist	349	160	6
46A	Nurse Administrator	424	125	6
71S	Special Investigations	4,370	4,370	6
42G	Physician Assistant	1,147	600	5
42N	Audiologist	133	0	5
43P	Pharmacist	292	268	5
43T	Biomedical Laboratory	270	190	5
48A	Aerospace Medicine Specialist	268	60	5
85G	United States Air Force Honor Guard	923	816	5
12F	Fighter Combat Systems Officer	1,730	1,551	4
13C	Special Tactics	263	0	4
17C	Cyberspace Operations Commander	729	0	4
20C	Logistics Commander	230	85	4
30C	Support Commander	1,412	365	4
42E	Optometrist	184	120	4
61B	Behavioral Scientist	1,366	821	4
61D	Physicist/Nuclear Engineer	206	130	4
65W	Cost Analyst	135	153	4
82A	Academic Program Manager	1,085	935	4
18S	Special Operations Remotely Piloted Aircraft Pilot	4,920	2,920	3
18X	RPA Pilot	430	365	3
42B	Physical Therapist	368	60	3
44G	General Practice Physician	530	320	3

Table A.2—Continued

AFSC	AFSC Title	Days Requested	Days Approved	Request Count
44M	Internist	30	10	3
44P	Psychiatrist	248	0	3
84H	Historian	910	574	3
96U	Unclassified Officer	1,267	847	3
10C	Operations Commander	279	125	2
11E	Experimental Test Pilot	825	0	2
12H	Rescue Combat Systems Officer	118	91	2
13L	Air Liaison Officer	395	1	2
18R	Reconnaissance Remotely Piloted Aircraft Pilot	1,050	511	2
43E	Bioenvironmental Engineer	730	0	2
46S	Operating Room Nurse	74	74	2
86P	Command and Control	270	150	2
91W	Wing Commander	304	0	2
95A	Non-Extended Active Duty U.S. Air Force Reserve Academy Liaison Officer	5,772	5,283	2
12E	Experimental Test Combat Systems Officer	150	0	1
18A	Attack Remotely Piloted Aircraft Pilot	30	30	1
40C	Medical Commander Health Services Utilization	30	0	1
43A	Aerospace and Operational Psychologist	180	180	1
44E	Emergency Services Physician	340	340	1
44R	Diagnostic Radiologist	30	30	1
81C	Training	1,168	1,168	1
96V	Unallotted	330	231	1
99A, 99X, 00X0	Unspecified AFSC	1,111,527	347,881	515
Total	107	3,571,013	1,098,815	4,195

SOURCE: Beast table in M4S data set.

References

AFI—*See* Air Force Instruction.

Air Force Instruction 36-2132, *Volume 2, Active Guard/Reserve (AGR) Program*, February 10, 2014.

Air Force Instruction 36-2619, *Military Personnel Appropriation Man-Day Program*, July 18, 2014.

Air Force Instruction 36-2629, *Individual Reservist Management*, August 13, 2012.

Air Force Instruction 2254, *Volume 1, Reserve Personnel Participation*, May 26, 2010.

Air Force Personnel Center, "Employment Categories, Manning" spreadsheet, fiscal year 2017, Not available to the general public.

Air National Guard, "History," webpage, undated. As of May 2, 2018: https://www.goang.com/discover-ang/history

Air Reserve Personnel Center, "A Look Back at Desert Storm," HQ Air Force Reserve Command Public Affairs, January 14, 2016. As of May 24, 2018: http://www.arpc.afrc.af.mil/News/Article-Display/Article/643429/a-look-back-at-desert-storm/

ANG—*See* Air National Guard.

Chief National Guard Bureau Manual 1302.01, *Orders Guidance for Counter Drug Aviation Personnel Migrating to Support Enhanced Southwest Border Security Operations*, July 26, 2013.

Crossland, Richard B., and James T. Currie, *Twice the Citizen: A History of the United States Army Reserve, 1908–1983*, Washington, D.C.: Office of the Chief, Army Reserve, 1984.

Currie, James T., and Richard B. Crossland, *Twice the Citizen: A History of the United States Army Reserve, 1908–1995*, Washington, D.C.: Department of the Army, 1997.

DA Cir. No. 103/DAF Letter 35-124, "Subj: Air Force Reserve and Air Force Honorary Retirees," April 14, 1948, MFA4002, AFRES.

Defense Travel Management Office, "Defense Travel System Modernization and Sustainment Initiatives," slide deck, 2017a. As of March 3, 2021: https://www.defensetravel.dod.mil/Docs/GovTravels_DTS_Modernization_and_Sustainmnent.pdf

———, "The New Joint Travel Regulations," 2017 GovTravels Symposium, March 1, 2017b.

Department of Defense Directive 1200.17, *Managing the Reserve Components as an Operational Force*, October 29, 2008.

Department of Defense Instruction 1205.18, *Full-Time Support (FTS) to the Reserve Components*, June 5, 2020.

Department of Defense Instruction 1215.06, *Uniform Reserve, Training, and Retirement Categories for the Reserve Components*, March 11, 2014.

Department of Defense Office of Legislative Counsel, Sixth Package of Legislative Proposals Sent to Congress for Inclusion in the National Defense Authorization Act for Fiscal Year 2016, sent to Congress on April 10, 2015 [Sec. 517. Expansion of Authorized Primary Duties of Air Force Reserve Component Full-Time Support Personnel].

Department of Defense Regulation 7000.14-R, *Department of Defense Financial Management Regulation*, Volume 11a, Reimbursable Options Policy, Chapter 3, Economy Act Orders, September 2019. As of March 3, 2021: https://comptroller.defense.gov/FMR/

DoD—*See* U.S. Department of Defense.

DoDI—*See* Department of Defense Instruction.

Dolfini-Reed, Michelle, and Darlene E. Stafford, *Identifying Duty Status Reforms Needed to Support an Operational Reserve*, Alexandria, Va.: Center for Naval Analyses, CRM D0021656.A2, 2010.

Doubler, Michael D., *Civilian in Peace, Soldier in War: The Army National Guard, 1636–2000*, Lawrence, Kan.: University Press of Kansas, 2003.

Doubler, Michael D., John W. Listman, and Donald M. Goldstein, *The National Guard: An Illustrated History of America's Citizens-Soldiers*, Dulles, Va.: Brassey's, 2003.

Duncan, Stephen M., *Citizen Warriors: America's National Guard and Reserve Forces & the Politics of National Security*, Novato, Calif.: Presidio Press, 1997.

Goffman, Edward M., "The Duality of the American Military Tradition: A Commentary," *Journal of Military History*, Vol. 64, No. 4, October 2000, pp. 967–980.

Halberstam, David, *The Best and the Brightest*, New York: Random House, 1972.

Headquarters Individual Reservist Readiness Integration Organization, "About HQ Rio," n.d. As of July 20, 2022: https://www.hqrio.afrc.af.mil/About/HQ-RIO/

Headquarters, United States Air Force, Office of Policy Integration, *2014 United States Air Force Reserve Handbook*, 2014.

Kapp, Lawrence, *Involuntary Reserve Activations for U.S. Military Operations Since World War II*, Washington, D.C.: Congressional Research Service, 2000.

———, *Reserve Component Personnel Issues: Questions and Answers*, Washington, D.C.: Congressional Research Service, July 2010.

Marine Administrative Message 469/15, *Procedures Concerning Reserve Marines Serving on Active Duty Operational Support (ADOS) Orders for More Than Three Years Within the Preceding Four-Year Period (1,095 Rule)*, September 24, 2015.

National Commission on the Structure of the Air Force, *Report to the President and Congress of the United States*, Arlington, Va., January 30, 2014.

National Guard, "25th Anniversary: Operation Desert Storm," webpage, 2016. As of May 24, 2018:
http://www.nationalguard.mil/Features/2016/Desert-Storm/

NCSAF—*See* National Commission on the Structure of the Air Force.

Office of the Air Force Judge Advocate, "Legal Review—Allowing Reserve Component (RC) Members to Provide Force Support Squadron (FSS) Services to Active Component (AC) Members," July 19, 2013.

Office of the Secretary of Defense, Total Force Policy Group, *Total Force Policy Report to Congress*, Washington, D.C., December 31, 1990.

Office of the Vice Chairman of the Joint Chiefs of Staff and Office of the Assistant Secretary of Defense for Reserve Affairs, *Comprehensive Review of the Future Role of the Reserve* Component, Washington, D.C.: Department of Defense, 2011.

Public Law 80-253, National Security Act of 1947, July 26, 1947. As of March 3, 2021:
https://www.hsdl.org/?view&did=2787

Public Law 108-375, Ronald W. Reagan National Defense Authorization Act for Fiscal Year 2005, October 28, 2004. As of March 3, 2021:
https://www.govinfo.gov/app/details/PLAW-108publ375

Public Law 109-163, National Defense Authorization Act for Fiscal Year 2006, January 6, 2006. As of March 3, 2021:
https://www.govinfo.gov/app/details/PLAW-109publ163

Public Law 110-181, National Defense Authorization Act for Fiscal Year 2008, January 28, 2008. As of November 15, 2021:
https://www.govinfo.gov/app/details/PLAW-110publ181

Public Law 112-81, National Defense Authorization Act for Fiscal Year 2012, Section 631, December 31, 2011. As of November 15, 2021:
https://www.govinfo.gov/app/details/PLAW-112publ81

Public Law 112-239, National Defense Authorization Act for Fiscal Year 2013, January 2, 2013. As of March 3, 2021:
https://www.govinfo.gov/app/details/PLAW-112publ239

Public Law 114-92, National Defense Authorization Act for Fiscal Year 2016, November 25, 2015. As of March 3, 2021:
https://www.govinfo.gov/app/details/PLAW-114publ92

Public Law 114-328, National Defense Authorization Act for Fiscal Year 2017, December 23, 2016. As of March 3, 2021:
https://www.govinfo.gov/app/details/PLAW-114publ328

Public Law 115-31, Consolidated Appropriations Act, 2017, Division C, Department of Defense Appropriations Act, 2017, May 5, 2017. As of March 3, 2021:
https://www.govinfo.gov/app/details/PLAW-115publ31

Public Law 115-91, National Defense Authorization Act for Fiscal Year 2018, December 12, 2017. As of March 3, 2021:
https://www.govinfo.gov/app/details/PLAW-115publ91

Reserve Forces Policy Board, Information Memo from MajGen Arnold Panuro, USMCR (Ret), Chairman, Reserve Policy Board, "Report of the Reserve Forces Policy Board on the 'Operational Reserve' and Inclusion of the Reserve Components in Key Department of Defense (DoD) Processes," January 14, 2013, pp. 1–2.

———, *Improving the Total Force: Using the National Guard and Reserves*, Falls Church, Va.: Office of the Secretary of Defense, November 2016.

RFPB—*See* Reserve Forces Policy Board.

Robbert, Albert A., James H. Bigelow, John E. Boon, Jr., Lisa M. Harrington, Michael McGee, S. Craig Moore, Daniel M. Norton, and William W. Taylor, *Suitability of Missions for the Air Force Reserve Components*, Santa Monica, Calif.: RAND Corporation, RR-429-AF, 2014. As of March 3, 2021:
https://www.rand.org/pubs/research_reports/RR429.html

Rohn, Laurinda L., Agnes Gereben Schaefer, Gregory A. Schumacher, Jennifer Kavanagh, Caroline Baxter, and Amy Grace Donohue, *Integrating Active and Reserve Component Staff Organizations: Improving the Chances of Success*, Santa Monica, Calif.: RAND Corporation, RR-1869-OSD, 2019. As of March 3, 2021:
https://www.rand.org/pubs/research_reports/RR1869.html

Schaefer, Agnes Gereben, John D. Winkler, Kimberly Jackson, Daniel Ibarra, Darrell D. Jones, and Geoffrey McGovern, *Approaches for Strengthening Total Force Culture and Facilitating Cross-Component Integration in the U.S. Military*, Santa Monica, Calif.: RAND Corporation, RR-2143-OSD, 2020. As of March 3, 2021:
https://www.rand.org/pubs/research_reports/RR2143.html

Sorley, Lewis, "Creighton Abrams and Active-Reserve Integration in Wartime," *Parameters*, Vol. 21, Summer 1991, pp. 35–50.

———, "Reserve Components: Looking Back to Look Ahead," *Joint Forces Quarterly*, Vol. 36, 1st Quarter 2005, pp. 18–23.

Stewart, Richard W., ed., *American Military History*, Volume II: *The United States Army in a Global Era, 1917–2003*, Washington, D.C.: Department of the Army, Center for Military History, 1989.

U.S. Code, Title 5, Government Organization and Employees; Part III, Employees; Subpart D, Pay and Allowances; Chapter 55, Pay Administration; Subchapter IV, Dual Pay and Dual Employment; Section 5538, Nonreduction in Pay While Serving in the Uniformed Services or National Guard. As of March 3, 2021:
https://uscode.house.gov/view.xhtml?req=granuleid:USC-prelim-title5
-section5538&num=0&edition=prelim

———, Title 5, Government Organization and Employees; Part III, Employees; Subpart E, Attendance and Leave; Chapter 63, Leave; Subchapter II, Other Paid Leave; Section 6323, Military Leave; Reserves and National Guardsmen. As of March 3, 2021:
https://www.govinfo.gov/app/details/USCODE-2010-title5/USCODE-2010
-title5-partIII-subpartE-chap63-subchapII-sec6323

———, Title 10, Armed Forces; Subtitle A, General Military Law; Part I, Organization and General Military Powers; Chapter 1, Definitions; Section 101, Definitions. As of March 3, 2021:
https://www.govinfo.gov/app/details/USCODE-2011-title10/USCODE-2011
-title10-subtitleA-partI-chap1-sec101

———, Title 10, Armed Forces; Subtitle A, General Military Law; Part I, Organization and General Military Powers; Chapter 2, Department of Defense; Section 115, Personnel Strengths: Requirement for Annual Authorization. As of March 3, 2021:
https://www.govinfo.gov/app/details/USCODE-2011-title10/USCODE-2011
-title10-subtitleA-partI-chap2-sec115

———, Title 10, Armed Forces; Subtitle E, Reserve Components; Part I, Organization and Administration; Chapter 1003, Reserve Components Generally; Section 10102, Purpose of Reserve Components. As of March 3, 2021:
https://www.govinfo.gov/app/details/USCODE-2011-title10/USCODE-2011
-title10-subtitleE-partI-chap1003-sec10102

———, Title 10, Armed Forces; Subtitle E, Reserve Components; Part I, Organization and Administration; Chapter 1003, Reserve Components Generally; Section 10103, Basic Policy for Order into Federal Service. As of March 3, 2021:
https://www.govinfo.gov/app/details/USCODE-2011-title10/USCODE-2011
-title10-subtitleE-partI-chap1003-sec10103

———, Title 10, Armed Forces; Subtitle E, Reserve Components; Part I, Organization and Administration; Chapter 1007, Administration of Reserve Components; Section 10216, Military Technicians (Dual Status). As of March 3, 2021
https://www.govinfo.gov/app/details/USCODE-2009-title10/USCODE-2009 -title10-subtitleE-partI-chap1007-sec10216

———, Title 10, Armed Forces; Subtitle E, Reserve Components; Part II, Personnel Generally; Chapter 1209, Active Duty; Section 12301, Reserve Components Generally. As of November 15, 2021:
https://www.govinfo.gov/app/details/USCODE-2011-title10/USCODE-2011 -title10-subtitleE-partII-chap1209-sec12301

———, Title 10, Armed Forces; Subtitle E, Reserve Components; Part II, Personnel Generally; Chapter 1209, Active Duty; Section 12304, Selected Reserve and Certain Individual Ready Reserve Members; Order to Active Duty Other Than During War or National Emergency. As of March 3, 2021:
https://www.govinfo.gov/app/details/USCODE-2011-title10/USCODE-2011 -title10-subtitleE-partII-chap1209-sec12304

———, Title 10, Armed Forces; Subtitle E, Reserve Components; Part II, Personnel Generally; Chapter 1209, Active Duty; Section 12310, Reserves: For Organizing, Administering, etc., Reserve Components. As of March 3, 2021:
https://www.govinfo.gov/app/details/USCODE-2010-title10/USCODE-2010 -title10-subtitleE-partII-chap1209-sec12310

———, Title 10, Armed Forces; Subtitle E, Reserve Components; Part II, Personnel Generally; Chapter 1209, Active Duty; Section 12314, Reserves: Kinds of Duty. As of March 3, 2021:
https://www.govinfo.gov/app/details/USCODE-2015-title10/USCODE-2015 -title10-subtitleE-partII-chap1209-sec12314

———, Title 10, Armed Forces; Subtitle E, Reserve Components; Part II, Personnel Generally; Chapter 1217, Miscellaneous Rights and Benefits; Section 12602, Members of Army National Guard of United States and Air National Guard of United States: Credit for Service as Members of National Guard. As of March 3, 2021:
https://www.govinfo.gov/app/details/USCODE-2010-title10/USCODE-2010 -title10-subtitleE-partII-chap1217-sec12602

———, Title 31, Money and Finance; Subtitle II, The Budget Process; Chapter 13, Appropriations; Subchapter I, General; Section 1301, Application. As of March 3, 2021:
https://www.govinfo.gov/app/details/USCODE-2010-title31/USCODE-2010 -title31-subtitleII-chap13-subchapI-sec1301

————, Title 31, Money and Finance; Subtitle II, The Budget Process; Chapter 13, Appropriations; Subchapter III, Limitations, Exceptions, and Penalties; Section 1341, Limitations on Expending and Obligating Amounts. As of March 3, 2021: https://www.govinfo.gov/app/details/USCODE-2011-title31/USCODE-2011 -title31-subtitleII-chap13-subchapIII-sec1341

————, Title 31, Money and Finance; Subtitle II, The Budget Process; Chapter 13, Appropriations; Subchapter III, Limitations, Exceptions, and Penalties; Section 1350, Criminal Penalty. As of March 3, 2021: https://www.govinfo.gov/app/details/USCODE-2011-title31/USCODE-2011 -title31-subtitleII-chap13-subchapIII-sec1350

————, Title 31, Money and Finance; Subtitle II, The Budget Process; Chapter 15, Appropriation Accounting; Subchapter II, Apportionment; Section 1517, Prohibited Obligations and Expenditures. As of March 3, 2021: https://www.govinfo.gov/app/details/USCODE-2010-title31/USCODE-2010 -title31-subtitleII-chap15-subchapII-sec1517

————, Title 32, National Guard; Chapter 1, Organization; Section 102, General Policy. As of March 3, 2021: https://www.govinfo.gov/app/details/USCODE-2010-title32/USCODE-2010 -title32-chap1-sec102

————, Title 32, National Guard; Chapter 3, Personnel; Section 328, Active Guard and Reserve Duty: Governor's Authority. As of March 3, 2021: https://www.govinfo.gov/app/details/USCODE-2011-title32/USCODE-2011 -title32-chap3-sec328

————, Title 32, National Guard; Chapter 5, Training; Section 502, Required Drills and Field Exercises. As of November 15, 2021: https://www.govinfo.gov/app/details/USCODE-2011-title32/USCODE-2011 -title32-chap5-sec502

————, Title 32, National Guard; Chapter 5, Training; Section 501, Training Generally. As of November 18, 2021: https://www.govinfo.gov/app/details/USCODE-2011-title32/USCODE-2011 -title32-chap5-sec501

————, Title 32, National Guard; Chapter 7, Service, Supply, and Procurement; Section 709, Technicians: Employment, Use, Status. As of March 3, 2021: https://www.govinfo.gov/app/details/USCODE-2011-title32/USCODE-2011 -title32-chap7-sec709

————, Title 37, Pay and Allowances of the Uniformed Services; Chapter 17, Miscellaneous Rights and Benefits; Section 910, Replacement of Lost Income: Involuntarily Mobilized Reserve Component Members Subject to Extended and Frequent Active Duty Service. As of March 3, 2021: https://www.govinfo.gov/app/details/USCODE-2010-title37/USCODE-2010 -title37-chap17-sec910

U.S. Constitution, Article I, Section 8, Clauses 1, 11, 12, 13, 15, 16.

U.S. Constitution, Article II, Section 2, Clause 1.

U.S. Department of Defense, *Report of the Eleventh Quadrennial Review of Military Compensation: Main Report*, Washington, D.C., June 2012.

———, *Report of the Military Compensation and Retirement Modernization Commission: Final Report*, January 2015.

———, *The Joint Travel Regulations: Uniformed Service Members and DoD Civilian Employees*, July 1, 2018.

U.S. Government Accountability Office, *DoD Joint Travel Regulations Actions Are Needed to Clarify Flat Rate Per Diem Policy*, Washington, D.C., GAO-17-353, May 2017.

Wexford Group International, *Reserve Component Military Duty Status Study: Considerations on Changing the Reserve Component Duty Status System (Phase II, Task 1)*, May 31, 2002.